Military Writers Society of America

SNAPSHOTS

AN ANTHOLOGY

August, 2023

SENIOR EDITOR: DWIGHT ZIMMERMAN

CONTRIBUTING EDITORS: BOB DOERR, ANGEL GIACOMO, AND JOAN RAMIREZ

COVER ART BY SANDRA LINHART

10 9 8 7 6 5 4 3 2

PUBLISHED IN THE UNITED STATES.

DEDICATION

To veterans and their families, and to those who gave the last full measure of devotion, whose memory we continue to honor.

INTRODUCTION

T HIS YEAR THE MILITARY WRITERS Society of America celebrates its twentieth anniversary. Founded by Vietnam War veteran Bill McDonald in 2003 as an outgrowth of his website and outreach efforts to veterans, the Military Writers Society of America is a national non-profit volunteer organization. We are a diverse group of authors: active-duty military, veterans, and civilians. We are historians, journalists, memoirists, bloggers, poets, musicians, and novelists. Some are old pros. Others are putting metaphorical or literal pen to paper for the first time. And then there are a majority somewhere in between. A love of the United States military binds us together as colleagues and friends.

As part of its service to members, MWSA provides publishing opportunities that might otherwise be unavailable to writers aspiring for a career as authors and that can be used as a stepping stone to obtain further work in the industry. One such venue is *Dispatches*, the organization's quarterly magazine. The other is the organization's anthologies. The latter include volumes published in conjunction with our annual conference.

The theme for this year's anthology is *Snapshots*. Like snapshot photographs that present a visual moment in life, the submissions in this volume offer text counterparts. The scope and variety of work presented in this volume are a testament to the quality and diversity of our membership.

Once again, submissions ran the gamut of genres and formats. They include memoirs devoted to everything from mundane life in the Vietnam war zone (not an oxymoron) to the most harrowing terror of being caught in the middle of a military coup in Myanmar. There are poetry and excerpts from work-in-progress novels, articles and short stories with their rich diversity of non-fiction and fiction themes.

I want to take a moment to extend my appreciation to everyone behind the scenes who helped make this year's anthology possible, starting with my fellow volunteer editors, Bob Doerr, Angel Giacomo, and Joan Ramirez. The four of us had the pleasure of being the first to see the submissions and to do the final editing necessary to make them ready for publication.

We want to give a special thanks to our copy editor and layout design artist, Ms. Sandra Linhart who did an outstanding job ensuring our edits were complete and we had a production-ready manuscript with a professional layout.

To all of our authors and volunteers, thank you for your hard work and a job well done.

Now, enjoy.

Dwight Zimmerman

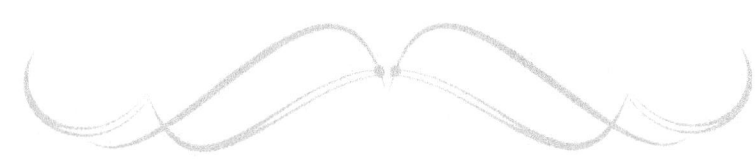

TABLE OF CONTENTS

SNAKE MAN

Ross Irvin

A Company, 1/8th Cav, 1st Cavalry Division, Ft Hood, TX

MARIA FLORES, DRESSED IN HER dowdy maid outfit, slowly unlocked the door to room 121 at the Bachelor Officers Quarters (BOQ), Ft Hood, Texas, then quickly pulled her cleaning cart inside. The occupant, a 2LT Killian, (name conveniently located on a card below his room number) had already lived there for several months. As expected, he was absent at work, so the small room smelled of stale air and yet curiously mixed with some aftershave.

Irish Spring, she thought. Her sharp brown eyes scanned the room, missing nothing.

As an inconspicuous bystander, Maria's aged brain retained a wealth of secret information on each of her charges from her weekly visits. For example, Lt Killian actually tried to keep a neat place. His bed was made. The olive-drab towel hung on the bathroom rack rather than crumpled on the floor. His underwear and socks were slapped together, out of sight in his government-issued chest of drawers. The trash, always an indicator of life-style, contained only two beer cans and some fast-food paper wraps. She noted there had never been any condoms, prophylactics, or drug paraphernalia.

SNAPSHOTS

As she wiped the porcelain sink in the tiny bathroom, she thought she heard a sound coming from the bedroom. She slowly peeped around the corner. There was a gentle rustling sound emanating from the opposite corner of the bed in one of four small cardboard boxes she had previously ignored.

What's that? she thought. She knelt next to the box then slowly opened the lid.

The box appeared to be partially filled with straw. She could barely make out a small cup of water. As she brought her face closer to peer into the further reaches of the box, there was fast movement.

The black head of a snake suddenly burst out inches from her nose. Its thin, pink tongue flicked in and out.

Maria screamed.

Her rag flew up into the air. She raced in terror from the room.

Where's the phone? She shook in her panic and impatience.

* * *

Somewhere in the Fort Hood 340-square-mile training area:

"Sir, we just got a strange call from the rear. Lieutenant Killian has to go back right away. There's some problem at the BOQ." Sgt Curtis dutifully extended his arm with the handset.

I was busily completing an operations order for a meeting in ten minutes, so 1SGT (Top) Simmons took the call.

I overheard, "Really? Really? Okay, we'll send him back right away."

"What's that all about?" I curiously asked.

Top Simmons, understanding priorities adroitly answered, "Why don't you keep Lieutenant Killian here after the meeting? It's not that big of a deal. I'll brief you about this after it."

The briefing about our company operation for that evening took about twenty minutes. In it, I assigned the objectives for the platoons and the company mortar section. At the end, I asked Lt Killian to remain behind and meet me in five minutes in the headquarters tent.

I entered the headquarters tent. Top Simmons was ready.

"Apparently Lieutenant Killian has been keeping live snakes in his BOQ room. A maid opened one of the boxes and one snake escaped. No maid, maintenance, or facilities management person will now enter the building until he gets rid of them."

I was shocked. I thought I had heard everything.

"Now what?" I hesitated. "I guess we'll have to get him back right away, so he'll be available this evening."

"Use my *Jeep*." Top Simmons quickly pulled up the flap of the tent and disappeared.

SNAPSHOTS

I called in Lt Killian. "Lieutenant, we have received a call from facilities management that you have been keeping snakes in your BOQ room. Get rid of them. My *Jeep* is waiting for you outside. When you get back, report to me."

"Yes, sir." Lt Killian saluted and left.

It had always been my policy not to get too involved in the personal lives of those who worked for me, especially lieutenants. As long as they were capable of performing their jobs, I wasn't particularly interested to find out if they drank, were bisexual, involved with the colonel's wife, or whatever. Still, I was curious about Lt Killian.

I knew Top didn't have the same restrictive scruples. He knew everything about everyone.

"So Top, tell me about Lieutenant Killian."

"Well sir, he is a herpetologist who somehow ended up in the infantry. He is fascinated by snakes and spends most of his spare time catching, studying, and releasing them. On his leave before he arrived here, he was in the big West Texas Rattlesnake Roundup. That's the contest in which you spend a day in the desert catching rattlesnakes. You earn prizes for capturing the longest snake, the largest number of snakes, the heaviest snake, etc. Apparently, he won the prize for the second longest snake."

"How does he catch them?"

"He has one of those water guns which he fills with gasoline instead of water. He crawls around the cliffs and sprays gasoline into the cracks. The vapor drives the snakes out. Lieutenant Killian has an elastic noose which he uses to catch the snake and release it into a bag. It's really pretty simple. By the way, his troops call him 'Snake Man'."

Three hours later, Lt Killian reported in then returned to his platoon. I thought it was the end of it, but I was wrong yet again.

"Sir, we just got another call from the rear. It's about Lieutenant Killian and the BOQ problem." Sgt Curtis again extended his arm with the handset.

That time I took the call.

"I'll look into this and get back to you," I promised. "Call Lieutenant Killian tell him to report here ASAP."

When he reported, Lt Killian looked confused.

"What's the problem, sir?"

"Well, the maid went back to your room. When she opened the door, she saw all the boxes were open. She was afraid to go in because of the snakes, so she called facilities management."

Killian laughed. "I left the boxes open to show there were no snakes in them. There aren't any in my room. They're non-poisonous anyway."

I quickly returned the call to facilities management. Another problem solved.

As Killian buckled up to go back to his platoon, I was curious about one omitted detail.

"So, lieutenant, what did you do with the snakes, then?" I casually asked. "Do you have a deal with a pet store?"

"No sir. I released them out the back door of the BOQ. They crawled under the building."

SNAPSHOTS

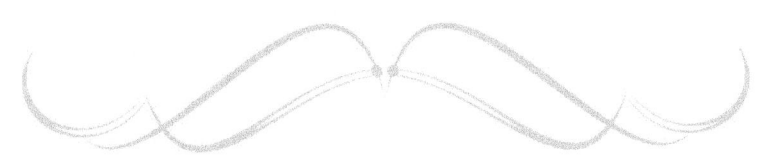

ROSS IRVIN IS A 1968 West Point graduate who served in Vietnam as a rifle platoon leader. He eventually served over twenty-nine years in the military through active duty, the New York Army National Guard, and the US Army Reserve, retiring as a colonel in 1998.

In 1991, as a student, he won the Army War College Foundation Award for best writing. He has been a contributor to the three *Both Sides of the Wall* anthologies about the West Point Class of 1968, as well as two anthologies for the Carrollton League of Writers, a local writers' organization.

Presently, he writes articles about coins and medals for *The California Numismatist* and *Numismatics International Bulletin.* In 2019 he received a master's degree in creative writing from the University of North Texas.

Ross lives in Carrollton, Texas with his wife, Margaret, and two cats.

Li'l Joe's Failure

Tom Beard

NAVAL AVIATORS ARE MORE THAN just the sum of their air exploits—Li'l Joe, for instance. Marian Z. Haggard, his real name—well, not quite. A navy chief in boot camp changed his last name's spelling because that, "...dip sh*t hillbilly didn't know how to spell."

His legal name heretofore ended in a T, and no one dared ever asked what the "Z" stood for. But that's another story for another time.

Li'l Joe was a little shorter in stature than most, but he stood taller than all in his abilities to lead—most of the time.

Li'l Joe was one of the Navy's best pilots (undisputed among his peers), a master lecturer in the classroom, and a leader of unparalleled skills during the 1950s and 60s—a Pied Piper among troops.

Li'l Joe, incidentally, on his first tour in A-1 *Skyraiders*, compiled over 2,000 hours in that formidable machine. A decade earlier, as a boy from the coal mining region of eastern Kentucky, he entered the Navy with a lie about his age, following early high school graduation thus escaping the inevitable mines.

Li'l Joe was designated an atomic weapons delivery pilot long before it was legal for him to drink alcohol.

SNAPSHOTS

His logbook as a lieutenant already revealed over 4,000 hours single-engine prop time when his qualities were abruptly transferred from cockpit to classroom.

When academic instructors wiled away time at their desks during lunches or between classes, Li'l Joe slipped off to the flight line volunteering to fly instructional flights.

Knowing they were flying with Li'l Joe, marginal students frequently flew their best flights. Students shuffling along the academic building's hallways openly expressed delight learning Li'l Joe was teaching their next class.

Thursday afternoons, once a month, was the traditional commanding officer's base inspection. The commanding officer didn't do it—he played golf. We lieutenants from academic training did by sharing various base sectors. The inspections frequently were superficial or non-existent depending on the inspecting officer's inclination or urge for early time off.

The off-base sewer farm landed one Thursday afternoon as Li'l Joe's assignment. The sewer tanks were unseen in the nearby woods. Few (I'd safely say, no "inspector") ever ventured down the red-clay road to the site to discover the base's unknown appendage.

Li'l Joe, typically, set off to do what no others ever did as the commanding officer's representative—to inspect the sewer farm. The caretaker, an eager elderly man, met Li'l Joe at the site. This ancient's job was to see the sewer's successful and continuous operation for this 'very important base training the world's best pilots', and always prepared for the never-to-happen commanding officer's inspection.

The keeper of the tanks waited a long, lonely vigil—likely since World War II—for a visit by the base's commanding officer to inspect his tanks. Now, it was happening. Li'l Joe, in full dress uniform, stood before him ready to inspect.

The keeper of the tanks was elated. For the following hour, the elder enthusiastically divulged to the "captain" everything he knew about that sewer system, captivating Li'l Joe.

But our hero met his defeat with the last exhibit.

The keeper fetched a tin cup hanging from a hook, dipped it into the watery stream flowing from the sewer's outlet, and from this cup took a hearty swallow.

That gesture was the keeper's proof to the commanding officer his system truly purified base sewer water before the tank's discharge joined the nearby creek leading off into the woods.

A bit stunned by that exhibit, Li'l Joe clumsily rejected the proffered, refilled tin cup and thus not officially affirming the plant's, or its manager's, success.

That was the one time Li'l Joe failed as a leader standing up to his full responsibilities as an exemplary naval officer and aviator.

SNAPSHOTS

TOM BEARD IS AUTHOR, EDITOR, and editor-in-chief of several books, writer of over a hundred journal articles, and writer of several chapters for others' books.

Four books authored by him received MWSA awards. Three were awarded gold and one bronze. Another book, as editor, received an MWSA gold. Other awards: *Admiral Arthur W. Radford Award For Excellence* in Naval Aviation History and Literature, voted writer of 2012 Best Article by *American Aviation History Journal* readers, and a Meritorious Public Service Award from the US Coast Guard Commandant for writings supporting Coast Guard history.

Additionally, Tom did a stint as a documentary film writer and editor, and he also served as a judge for the MWSA book contest.

Tom holds a MA degree in history with additional formal graduated studies in American maritime history. He split a twenty-year active military flying career as a Navy carrier attack pilot and a Coast Guard rescue pilot.

Tom and his wife, as a team, navigated sailboats nearly twice around the world over a sixteen-year period cruising over 160,000 miles, living at times in over thirty countries. Hobbies include rebuilding 100+-year-old cars, gardening, and writing.

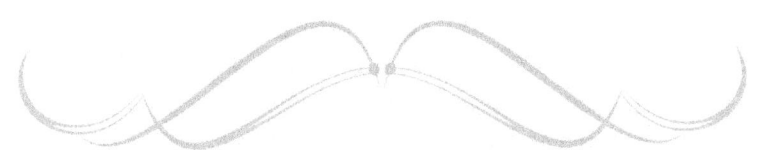

From a Chicken to an Eagle

Walter "Butch" Maki

In June 1967, supply convoys came under constant attack between Pleiku and Kontum Vietnam. To counter more losses, the 4th Infantry Division decided to send one of its companies to sweep the area.

I was a *Huey* crew chief, and we were assigned to support the company's third platoon. For two days, we flew 'ass and trash' without a shot fired. Ass being men and trash being supplies. On the third day, we picked up the evening meal's empty miramar cans and were on our way to return them to the 4th Division's base camp.

I was looking forward to a steak and the smooth scotch Russ, my gunner, won in a poker game against one of the supply guys.

Tired from loading ammo, water, and men since six o'clock that morning, I sat back and watched the setting sun cast shadows from palm trees and little hamlets where kids ran out to wave at us as we flew by.

At five hundred feet and one hundred knots it happened fast. It sounded like a five-pound hammer being slammed on the roof above our heads. Next, I heard an immediate coughing and tearing metal sound as the 1,300 horsepower of our engine goes *kamikaze*, and self-destructs.

"Oh, shit!" I said, as lights and alarms triggered the warning system's Christmas tree.

SNAPSHOTS

The gift under that tree was a freewheel clutch. A brilliant little device that had saved more air crews of rotary-winged aircraft than Sikorsky could have ever imagined. Without it, a helicopter with no engine power would have the aerodynamics of a wall safe.

Once that sucker disengaged from the main rotor shaft, the blades auto-rotated and we descended under collective pitch control where the pilot trades off RPMs for lift.

The result was the freewheeling rotors function as a *de facto* parachute.

The sudden descent sent my stomach into dizziness. At splash down in a rice paddy, my seat belt jerked around my waist. I heard miramar cans smash into the back of the pilot's seat, and others flew out the cabin doors.

Mud flew everywhere.

"One bullet worth about twenty-five cents just caused a three-hundred-thousand-dollar helicopter to become stuck in the mud," I muttered in disgust.

"Maybe this is more than just a lucky shot," Warrant Officer JD, our co-pilot, observed, as he pointed to a VC squad at the opposite end of the rice paddy. "I couldn't get anyone on the radio after our engine conked out, and now no one answers on the emergency freq."

"Try the company freq," Aircraft Commander Captain Montgomery said as Russ racked his M60, waiting for the Cong to advance.

"Mayday. Mayday. Any aircraft. This is Bikini one-four-four."

"*One-four-four, this is Drydock five,*" came an immediate response. "*What's up?*"

"Shit," I said. "It's Lieutenant Chickenshit Rose."

Rose was the night maintenance officer. He always wore freshly starched uniforms and was the only one in the company with spit-shined jump boots. His demeanor was that he was the king of the flight line at night.

Everybody knew he was afraid to fly combat missions. That was why Rose volunteered to be in charge of the night maintenance shift—the worst duty available to a commissioned officer. To make up for his lack of courage, he made it hell on every one of his subordinates and enlisted flight crews.

Montgomery got on and said, "Drydock five, we are twenty miles northwest of Pleiku, stuck in a rice paddy just west of route seven with a squad of VC closing in on us."

"*I'm on a test flight with no guns or crew,*" Rose responded. "*I'll try to raise someone in the area.*"

Rose called for help.

What seemed like forever but was most likely only a few minutes, he radioed "*Bikini-one-four-four, the closest help is thirty minutes out.*"

"Shit, we'll be dead by then," Russ quickly blurted out.

"Where the hell is Rose?" Montgomery questioned.

"Drydock five, what's your location?" JD inquired.

"*I'm within five miles of you.*"

Montgomery grabbed the mike and ordered, "Get your ass in here. Now!"

"He's not coming," I said, as I watched the edge of the rice paddy for signs of movement or firefly flashes in the weeds over the sights of my M16. "He has an inherent aversion to danger."

"Russ, get the M60s and M16s with all the ammo we can carry and come with me," Montgomery said. "Mack, put the rest of the ammo, guns, and radios in the center of the ship and turn on the fuel drains."

SNAPSHOTS

Captain Montgomery's order meant he was giving up hope that a *Chinook* could come to pull our bird out of the mud. Instead, we not only had to abandon our ship, but we had to destroy it, so it and its contents would not fall into enemy hands.

I felt a sadness, as I had grown attached to that bird. I had spent a lot of harrowing hours in it, countless hours inspecting it, and late nights maintaining it. Not to mention she delivered us back to earth without a scratch.

The VC were halfway across the rice patty and shooting. Montgomery and Russ returned fire from behind a dike. A noxious smell filled the air as soon as the leaking JP4 jet fuel added to the oil hitting the hot engine surfaces.

I suddenly heard the sound of a *Huey*.

"Did you get someone on the radio to rescue us?" I asked JD.

His answer gave me goosebumps all over when he said, "Rose."

I thought, Shit. Rose will not do an assault under enemy fire without gunship and door gun support. He positively will not land in this shit.

I looked up, and to my astonishment, I saw Rose in an approach to land.

And so did the VC.

Green tracers concentrated on the *Huey* while Russ and the captain tried to give as much suppressive fire as possible.

"Shit! Rose is getting pounded," JD exclaimed.

I told JD, "I'm not convinced he will continue through that much ground fire."

But he kept coming.

The aircraft landed. Russ, Montgomery, and JD ran for the *Huey*.

I pulled the pin on two hand grenades, tossed them in my ship, and ran for the rescue bird.

A few seconds later, I heard the grenades explode. As I approached Rose's *Huey*, I felt the heat on my back coming from my beloved bird's demise.

As soon as I jumped on board, Rose pulled pitch, and I was pushed to the back of the seat by the acceleration.

I sat there dumbfounded and a bit in shock. Rose saved our asses. I also was amazed at Rose's ability to keep the bird just inches above the paddy's dikes and close to Huey's top speed until we were clear of the VC's range of fire.

He then did a cyclic climb out.

A cyclic climb is when a chopper is at high speed, and the pilot pulls back on the cyclic stick, sacrificing airspeed for climb rate. That maneuver makes the helicopter soar like a home-sick angel.

At 5,000 feet, Rose leveled off.

SNAPSHOTS

Sir Isaac Newton's First Law—an object in motion stays in motion—took effect. My ass left the seat as we went from climbing at 4,000 feet per minute to level flight.

Once the aircraft was at altitude and cruising at eighty knots, Rose asked Captain Montgomery to take control of the aircraft.

Rose lifted his hand and said, "Look, I'm so scared, I'm shaking."

Montgomery's reply showed us he was a true leader and more than just our bad luck charm.

He said, "Courage isn't the absence of fear, just the mastering of it, and today, lieutenant, you overcame yours."

After we landed at Camp Holloway, our home base, I opened Montgomery's door and pushed back his armored seat plate. I could not help but notice that the window above Rose had a bullet hole, and the instrument panel had caught three rounds.

There was no denying it. Rose was getting hits all around him but kept his approach despite it.

After the rotor blades stopped, Rose took off his helmet. I went to his open door and said, "Thank you, lieutenant."

He nodded and leaned forward in his seat saying, "There's something poking me." He then pulled an AK47 round from the webbing below him.

"Lieutenant," I laughed and continued, "Your ass was so puckered while taking fire that the bullet couldn't penetrate it.

We all laughed at that.

SNAPSHOTS

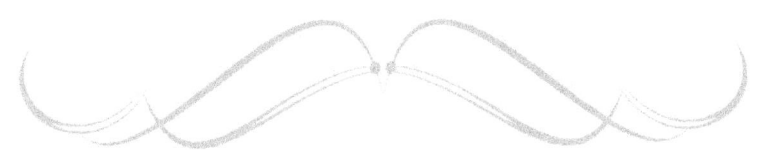

WALTER "BUTCH" MAKI READS LIKE a typical American story with many turns in his life.

From a decorated war veteran, turned blue-collar worker, turned political organizer, turned entrepreneur, and now an award-winning author.

But for this New Hampshire farm boy, he sees all that as "just doing my job".

He is now retired and writes as a hobby, with his first novel, *Bikini Beach*, due out in February.

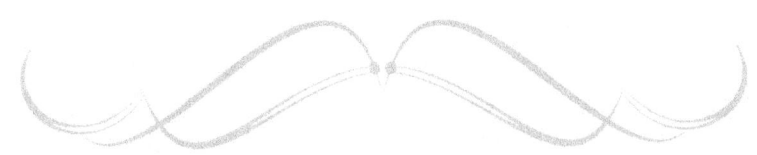

U-TURN

Ingo Kaufman

Author's note: The following excerpt is from an interview with Khalid (last name intentionally withheld), an Iraqi interpreter who spent almost five years working for the Coalition. Speaking nearly perfect English but tending to avoid the past tense in favor of the present, he spent six months with the author's armor company operating west of Fallujah in 2004, and another four years in Baghdad. Khalid's full story will appear in an upcoming book.

This account is about the two times Khalid met Saddam Hussein.

ONE DAY IN THE MID-NINETEEN-EIGHTIES, Khalid and his classmates received a special announcement.

"I was in middle school, sixth grade," he recalled. "The principal and the teachers were all saying, 'We have a big day today.' Everybody was looking at each other, 'What's going on?'

"They took us all outside, put us in line, and said, 'The president will come to this area and will visit the school and say hi to the kids.' The convoys started to come, all those fancy presidential *Mercedes*, or whatever they had at the time. They all looked the same."

Khalid and his classmates waited, whispering and wondering from which black car Saddam Hussein would emerge.

SNAPSHOTS

When the head of state stepped out, Khalid recalled, "He was wearing a white suit. Everybody was saying 'hi' to the president—all the kids. He walked by the sidewalk saying 'hi' to them, shaking their hands, and putting his hand on their heads. He walked by me, and he put his hand on top of my head."

Years passed. As Khalid grew up, life got more difficult. With a Persian Shiite father and an Iraqi Sunni mother, despite being born and raised in Iraq, he and his siblings faced a major hurdle.

"Saddam Hussein made a law saying, even if you were born there, you're not an Iraqi, because you follow your dad," Khalid said. "We spent a lifetime in Iraq with no citizenship because my dad was an Iranian citizen."

No citizenship meant no college and limited opportunities.

During the Persian Gulf War in 1991, Khalid's family left Baghdad and took refuge in the countryside. Iraq's defeat left its economy in ruins. Khalid spent the next decade desperately seeking work to avoid going hungry.

In late 2003, when the Americans offered him a position as an interpreter, he accepted the dangerous job. Not only did he want to help, but the monthly salary of six hundred dollars was more money than he had seen in his entire life.

In 2004, after proving his mettle for six months in a dangerous sector west of Fallujah, Khalid requested a transfer to Camp Victory near Baghdad International Airport. For the next two years, American military police units rotated in and out of Camp Victory while Khalid remained.

"Every year, I see new faces," he said. "One day, a new unit showed up. They came to escort me from the gate for a mission and introduced me to everybody. We rolled downtown and did a mission with the traffic police headquarters. When we came back, we drive through the IZ [International Zone]."

The convoy leader, a newly arrived captain, wanted to go to the embassy. No one knew the way—except for Khalid. The captain ordered the interpreter's *Humvee* to the front of the column to lead them through the Green Zone to their destination.

"We reached the embassy and I said in the radio, 'Hey, this is the embassy'."

"Why are we here?" the captain's voice crackled over the radio.

"You said 'the embassy'," Khalid replied.

"No, I meant the chow hall," came the response.

"Oh, you didn't say that. You said, 'the embassy'."

"Okay, where's the chow hall, then?".

Khalid informed them they had passed the chow hall, located on the same street, just moments before. As it was a cul-de-sac, they proceeded a bit further to make a U-turn when they encountered a strange sight.

SNAPSHOTS

"I saw a lot of people standing there waiting outside by the sidewalk—media guys carrying cameras. When our convoy stopped, they all came towards our vehicle."

"Hey, is he with you guys?" the journalists asked.

Khalid opened his door and inquired, "What's going on?"

"Are you guys escorting Saddam?"

"Escorting Saddam? Where?"

"To the court."

"Oh no, we're here by mistake. We're just doing a U-turn."

Saddam Hussein was about to stand trial. Unbeknownst to the newly arrived soldiers, the court was located on the same street as the chow hall, only a bit further down.

The journalists realized their error and retreated in disappointment while Khalid explained to the rest of the convoy what was happening and asked if anyone else wanted to stay and watch. Everyone declined, but Khalid asked if he could stay. Since he wasn't allowed to be alone, his crew remained with him while the rest of the convoy turned around and headed off to eat.

He stepped out of the *Humvee* and stood by the sidewalk. Moments later, another military convoy drove up, this one escorting an armored bus.

Dressed in his body armor, Kevlar helmet, and sunglasses, Khalid was barely distinguishable from the other soldiers. He was able to inch closer to the door of the bus.

"All of a sudden, *boom!* There he was."

Guards escorted the deposed dictator down the stairs of the bus and onto the sidewalk, right past the waiting Khalid.

So, in his local dialect, Khalid said, "What a coincidence. I saw you twice in my life."

Surprised, Hussein turned and looked at Khalid, slowly shook his head, and walked on.

"That was the second time—and the last time."

The court sentenced Hussein to death by hanging.

To this day, Khalid has never watched the leaked video of the execution. However, he reserves no nostalgic memories of the Iraq in which he grew up a second-class citizen, or of the man whose reign of terror lasted most of his lifetime.

"He lived as a coward and died as a coward. If anyone's saying the opposite...I don't want to use bad words," Khalid said.

As for the aloof captain who had something better to do, Khalid got to know him over the coming year and came to understand why he hadn't wanted to stay.

"I don't want to say it, but that captain—all the missions we did every day for a whole year, the most important thing for him is to go to the chow hall at the end."

If Khalid withheld bad words for a tyrant, he surely wouldn't criticize a hungry captain. In the end, the interpreter knew the convoy commander's nagging appetite and vague instructions had provided closure.

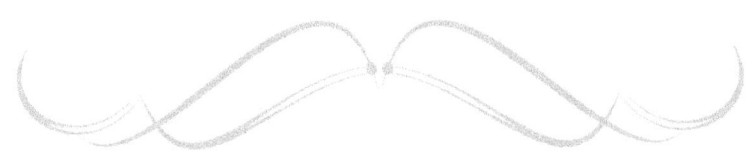

INGO KAUFMAN SERVED IN THE U.S. Army as a platoon leader in 2004 in Habbiniyah, Iraq, with 1-34 Armor, 1ˢᵗ Infantry Division, and as the division's 1ˢᵗ Brigade Combat Team's HHC executive officer in Fort Riley, Kansas until 2006.

Following his military service, the Michigan native worked in various logistical management, training, and engineering roles for two *Fortune 500* companies on two continents.

Before enlisting, he worked countless odd jobs: journalist, *American Red Cross* authorized training provider, translator, substitute teacher, English assistant in France, industrial clean up, cafeteria worker, hotel night security, and many more.

Ingo enjoys nature, reading, spending time with his wife and two children, and learning about autism. He is working on his first book, a collection of interviews and personal accounts from his time in Iraq.

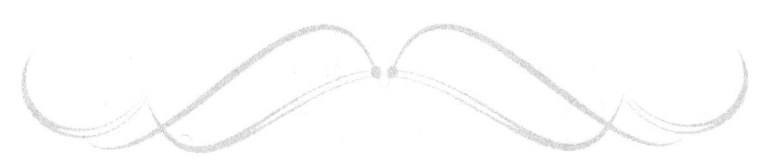

THE WRITE STUFF

Gary B. Zelinski

WHY WRITE? I'M REALLY NOT sure. Lillian, my wonderful bride of forty-eight years, and I have been recording our travels since 2007. Our blogs to family and friends were quick updates on our whereabouts rather than a serious attempt to string together a coherent story. Practice helped improve my prose, but the places were the real story. Pictures chronicled our adventures and were what everyone wanted, anyway.

So why, in retirement, have you decided to write and share your stories?

That's a good question. I wish I knew. Partly, I think I want to share memories, and partly I want to keep in touch with the people we've befriended. In the military and traveling in an RV, you are always leaving someone behind.

In my memoirs, I enjoyed reliving the exploits of three of my friends during my military years. None of them are as good as my memories, but therein lies the reality I want to remember.

Now that I've written a little about each of them, my stories have become the truth. At least, the truth for me.

Isn't life better that way?

SNAPSHOTS

I recently bought a new TV. One of those super-sharp, ultra-high-definition, flat-screen wonders. If you get up close, you can see every pore on everyone's face. This is reality run amok. I quickly discovered I needed to step back and not get too close. Maybe we don't need to see every detail to know the truth.

With writing, there need not be a blemish or imperfection. I like choosing the reality I want and ignoring the facts that only live on the surface.

A quick *Google* search yielded writing tips from America's best writers. According to Ernest Hemingway, you should use "vigorous English". I'm not sure what that means.

John Steinbeck advised, "Write freely and as rapidly as possible and throw the whole thing on paper." Now, that's solid advice, like all these ideas are somehow trapped in my brain and all I need is a keyboard for them to flood out.

William Faulkner wrote over 2,400 words about being a writer. This compared to Hemingway's fourteen. I guess Faulkner had a lot more to say. He did advise would-be authors to read, read, and read. Sadly, I don't. I think I should.

Stephen King said pretty much the same thing but then added, "don't watch television." Sadly, again, I do.

King went on to say that as a writer, you should master the art of description. His next tip was you shouldn't give too much background information. I'll try and incorporate those two jewels in my next story.

I have started to read and, in a few cases, reread classic American literature. Long overdue.

I enjoy writing from the aspect of telling a story. If ever I get good enough to offer some advice on writing, I think my first offering would be to make sure you have something interesting to say. I believe having a good story is more important than good grammar. People can help you with your grammar, but those same people can only confide the truth when it comes to your story.

"Your grammar is impeccable, but your story sucks."

I don't much care for fiction, sci-fi, fantasy, romance, mystery, or the true crime genres. Also, non-fiction tends to be boring or depressing. Lately, it has been both. Self-help is a waste of time, as are cookbooks without pictures.

Lillian says I should read *Alexander Hamilton* by Ron Chernow. She thinks I should read all 818 pages. I watched the play instead. It cost me twenty bucks on the *Disney* channel.

I got halfway through Obama's 768-page autobiography, *The Promised Land*. It took three credits on *Audible*.

It's not that I can't read. It's that I read slowly. My mind wanders. I feel guilty I'm not doing some household chore or working out. I've got to get into better shape. I can't wait for February. In February, I get to give up all the New Year's resolutions I made in January.

With writing, as opposed to real life, you can often simultaneously travel several courses. Why choose? And so, my following two writing projects will take their own paths.

After finishing my memoir, I struggled a bit with my next path. So, while Lillian labors away, turning my manuscript into a format suitable for publishing, I sit and ponder what's next.

One project I've been working on for several years is about my visits to Arlington National Cemetery. I'm trying to make enough trips to assemble a book with photographs and a bit of background on just a few of the heroes buried there.

The cemetery is huge, and with 400,000 souls resting there, it's a bit of a daunting task. It's also somber. I realize that a book about Arlington might not be

SNAPSHOTS

everyone's 'cup of tea', but I hope you will find the stories inspiring and leave you with a little more pride in our country than the nightly news might suggest.

My other and newest project directly results from the literary criticisms many have gracefully bestowed upon me. Unlike my Arlington project, this one will be anything but somber.

Some have suggested that I try my hand at fiction. As if my memoirs and making up tales from my mediocre past wasn't fiction enough. I'm endeavoring to create a collection of short stories and verbal cartoons, the likes of which have been told a million times before.

I very much don't like fiction. I don't read it and give it a good bash every chance I get. I've even gone so far as to deny fiction even exists. After all, fiction is just a set of facts that haven't happened yet.

My Arlington National Cemetery book is a labor of love. It takes time, photographs, and finding just enough facts to make each story interesting. For me, the stories of the heroes buried at Arlington are compelling and speak to some better people who, now in death, can teach us how precious our own lives are.

The writing is simple, straightforward, and comes easy.

On the other shoe, writing humorous fiction is anything but simple, straightforward, and easy. At best, the writing is obtuse, confusing to the humor-impaired, and often funny only to me.

Fiction writing is a multi-billion-dollar-a-year business. Tens of thousands of titles are annually published, with hundreds of thousands of books sold. Would-be authors compete tooth and nail (or pen and quill) for an opening on bestseller lists in every major newspaper. Fame is won or lost based on the reviews of a few so-called critics. Hungry new fiction writers dream of becoming the next Tom Clancy, Stephen King, or that Harry Potter woman.

The Handmaid's Tale is a creepy TV series written by a lovely old lady who wrote an even creepier book. Why? Why did she write it? Worse yet, why would anybody read it?

A best-selling fiction writer makes twelve times the money that a best-selling non-fiction writer makes. But the fiction writer competes in a world fifteen times larger. So why, with so much to be gained, is there so much bad fiction out there? Could it be possible? It just might be—it's all bad fiction?

Every story told has been told a hundred times before. The novelty of Shakespeare is that his stories are all way too familiar. Melville, Dickens, and Twain might have broken ground, but it was well-tended soil.

I just made up all the preceding facts. But, see, I'm getting the hang of fiction writing already.

I learned to write at the Air Force Academy. No, I didn't actually go to the Air Force Academy. Instead, they came to me.

I was a young airman on my first assignment on a small Strategic Bomber Base in Arkansas. The two-week writing class taught me everything I know.

SNAPSHOTS

Write as you speak. Have three main points. Tell them what you're going to tell them. Tell them, and then tell them again. I liked the part when they said it was okay to use contractions. I vowed to use a lot of contractions.

In the military, we lived by building and giving briefings.

"Oh, honey, you're upset? I'm so sorry. I promise to do better if you give me a twenty-seven-slide *PowerPoint* briefing on your feelings."

The Air Force taught me to be as brief as possible, while the CIA wanted thoroughness. I must have sat through hundreds of eighty-plus page agency slideshows where the point was lost back on page number forty-seven. No wonder it took eleven years to find Bin Laden.

In my last years as a consultant to senior government and military leaders, I learned to write as directly as possible. Time is a senior executive's greatest commodity. In executive communication, put the 'ask' on the first slide. I often never got past my first slide.

Nope, next.

Those were the most common responses I heard. For example, I once wrote a highly classified, super-secret letter for the director of the CIA. My draft made it through the staff of the NSA and the CIA. Nobody changed a word. Not one word. My boss was so impressed that I got a job writing speeches and correspondence for our director.

After some success, I decided that everyone in my office should only refer to me as Ernest. Ernest of Hemingway fame. When our chief of staff publicly told me Hemingway used to wear women's shoes, I quickly pivoted to Antonio.

Throughout 2022, some of my stories were published in *Dispatches* magazine.

Dispatches is the quarterly publication of the Military Writers Society of America. The first few articles came from my memoirs, *Aim High. A Love Story*. A few more came from my upcoming book about a few of the heroes buried at Arlington National Cemetery.

I am indebted to the MWSA and especially to Ms. Sandra Linhart, the editor of *Dispatches* magazine. Her encouragement fueled my articles, and her careful reviews made my incoherent musing a better read.

In 2023, I hope to publish both my memoirs and my Arlington book. If I make it over the finish line, it will be largely due to the mentorship and friendship of Sandra and others at MWSA.

SNAPSHOTS

WHEN YOU MEET SOMEONE AT age twelve, fall in love, and spend the next fifty years together, it's hard to know where one person starts and the other ends.

Gary B. Zelinski retired from the USAF after twenty-two years. His bride, Lillian, raised two delightful children and rose through the ranks to become a senior vice president for a *Fortune 500* tech company.

In 2020, his father passed away due to complications from dementia. It's not hereditary, but memories fade even for the best of us. His memoir, *Aim High, a Love Story*, will be published in 2023. His next book is about the heroes buried at Arlington National Cemetery.

When not on Grandpa duty, Gary writes to thank those who gave him more than he could give back and leave a little of who he was, not just what he did. *Retirement is hard enough, why not get paid?*

Dwight Eisenhower: America's First Pilot President

Penny Rafferty Hamilton, Ph.D.

IN 1916, THEN ARMY SECOND Lieutenant Dwight Eisenhower wanted to marry the young socialite, Mamie Doud. Mamie's father agreed to the marriage on the condition Eisenhower did not enter the Army Air Service, which Doud considered too dangerous. According to Merrill Atwater, President Eisenhower's great-grandson, the family story is Ike wanted to become a pilot much sooner.

"In 1916, when Ike's father-in-law told him, 'You can't marry my daughter and learn to be a pilot at the same time,' Ike complied." Atwater said that years later when Eisenhower was in the Philippines, Ike thought it would be okay to fly.

Eisenhower was a lieutenant colonel in the Philippines, serving under General Douglas MacArthur. One of Eisenhower's flight instructors was William L. "Jerry" Lee, who was training the pilots for the nascent Philippine Air Force.

According to the Eisenhower Presidential Museum, Ike learned to fly while stationed in the Army in the Philippines. Eisenhower soloed in a *Stearman* PT-1 on May 19, 1937. Later, he flew a *Stinson Reliant* and logged over 350 hours from July 1936 to November 1939.

SNAPSHOTS

Eisenhower's Presidential papers from 1916-52 also reveal Ike earned a private pilot license in 1939 at Fort Lewis in the State of Washington. That aviation knowledge was extremely important to Eisenhower in World War II planning as the supreme commander of allied forces.

As we look back seventy years to the 1953 presidency of Dwight Eisenhower, it is another opportunity to reflect on his unique place in our nation's aviation history as America's first pilot president.

According to research from Dan Ford at the Warbird's forum, a reference about flying in the post-Philippines period is found in *At Ease: Stories I Tell to Friends by Dwight D. Eisenhower* on page 227:

> *After World War II, I had ceased to fly altogether, except that once in a while, on a long trip, to relieve my boredom and demolish the pilot's, I would move into the co-pilot's seat and take over the controls. But as the jet age arrived, I realized that I had come out of a horse and buggy background, recognized my limitations, and kept to a seat in the back.*

In a November 2014, Akron Beacon Journal article, former Presidential pilot, Billy Draper, said, "The President sometimes came up to sit in the co-pilot's seat when we were flying." Draper became Eisenhower's personal pilot and Air Force aide on call 24/7 after Eisenhower's election in November 1952.

The National Museum of the US Air Force interestingly states:

> *The U-4B, a US Air force version of the Aero Commander l-26, was used by President Dwight D. Eisenhower from 1956 to 1960 for short trips. A pilot himself, President Eisenhower often took the controls, primarily during trips between Washington, DC and his farm in Gettysburg, PA. The first presidential aircraft to have only two engines, the U-4B was also the first presidential aircraft to carry the familiar blue-and-white-paint scheme.*

According to the National Museum of the US Air Force, this U-4B, which is the Air Force version of the Aero Commander L-26, was used by President Dwight Eisenhower. After he left office, this airplane was given to the Air Force Academy skydiving team in October 1969. The jumpers used it in Colorado Springs for parachute training. (United States Air Force)

First Lady Mamie Eisenhower, who was from Denver, named their presidential Constellation, *Columbine* as a tribute to the Colorado state flower. Over those years as the planes grew in size and power *Columbine II*, and even III, were also *Lockheed* Constellations.

Then, according to www.history.com, *Air Force One* became the official name of the President's plane.

> *While many think of **Air Force One** as the name of the President's airplane, **Air Force One** is a call sign applied to any aircraft carrying the American president. The name was created following an incident in 1953, when President Dwight D. Eisenhower's plane found it was using the same call sign (8610) as a nearby **Eastern Airlines** commercial flight. Eisenhower was our first President to travel aboard a plane designated **Air Force One**.*

Another aviation first was prompted by Eisenhower when in 1957 he suggested to Draper that a helicopter would be useful for shorter trips to and from the White House. The Secret Service agreed.

SNAPSHOTS

So, on July 12, 1957, Eisenhower became our first president to ride in a helicopter. A *Bell UH-13-J Sioux* was used to fly Ike to Camp David and his Gettysburg farm, eventually flying directly from the White House south lawn.

Mamie Eisenhower named the presidential Lockheed Constellation airplane, **Columbine***, after the Colorado state flower. (Library of Congress)*

According to *Wikipedia*, toward the end of Eisenhower's term in 1958, the Air Force added three *Boeing* 707 jets—VC-137s designated SAM 970, 971, and 972, into the fleet. Eisenhower became our first president to use the jet airplane during his "Flight to Peace" Goodwill tour from December 3 through 22, 1959.

He visited eleven Asian nations, flying 22,000 miles, about twice as fast as he could have covered that distance flying in one of the *Columbines*.

Eisenhower's aviation legacy was extensive. He was an important leader in the founding of the U.S. Air Force Academy.

The US Air Force Academy was established April 1, 1954, the culmination of an idea years in the making. Air power leaders, long before the Air Force was a separate service, argued the Air Force needed a dedicated school to educate Air Force officers.

After September 1947, when the Air Force was established as a separate service, that idea finally had the legitimacy of the new service behind it.

In 1948, the Air Force appointed the Stearns-Eisenhower board, named for its chairmen, Robert L. Stearns, president of the University of Colorado, and Dwight Eisenhower, president of Columbia University. They studied the existing military academies and the options for an Air Force Academy. Their conclusion was the Air Force needed its own academy.

After Congress passed a bill establishing the Air Force Academy, the secretary of the Air Force appointed a commission to recommend a location. After traveling 21,000 miles and considering hundreds of sites, the commission recommended Colorado Springs as its first choice. The Secretary agreed and the purchasing of the thousands of acres began.

The state of Colorado contributed $1 million to the purchase of the land. Today, that would be well over $12,000,000.

On July 11, 1955, the same year construction on the Academy began in Colorado Springs, the first class of 306 men was sworn-in at a temporary site on Lowry Air Force Base in Denver.

Lieutenant General Hubert R. Harmon, a key figure in the development of early plans for an Academy, was recalled from retirement by then President Dwight D. Eisenhower to become the first Air Force Academy superintendent.

In 1958, President Eisenhower also signed the Federal Aviation Act which transferred responsibility from the old

SNAPSHOTS

Civil Aeronautics Authority to the newly created Federal Aviation Administration (FAA). Air Force General Elwood "Pete" Quesada became the very first FAA Administrator.

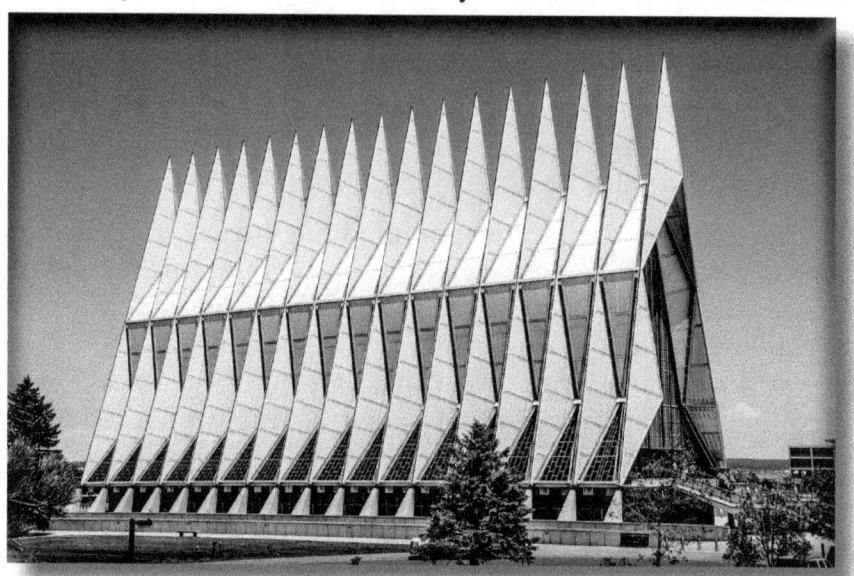

Although Eisenhower was born in Denison, TX, he always considered Kansas his home. His boyhood home, Presidential Library, and final resting place are in Abilene.

In 2014, Kansas paid tribute to our pilot president, by renaming that state's largest and busiest airport, Dwight D. Eisenhower National Airport in Wichita, Kansas, called the Air Capital of the World.

Today, the former Wichita Mid-Continent Airport (KICT) main road is renamed Eisenhower Airport Parkway, too.

Since 1937, when Dwight D. Eisenhower first learned to fly, he saw many changes in aviation—jets, supersonic airplanes, and the beginning of space exploration.

Always the visionary, in 1958, President Eisenhower signed the legislation creating our National Aeronautics and Space Administration (NASA).

Since Dwight Eisenhower "Flew West" in 1969, we have been shown moon landings, spacewalks, drones, and now autonomous airplanes.

Eisenhower once said, "Accomplishment will prove to be a journey not a destination."

That is so true in aviation and aerospace.

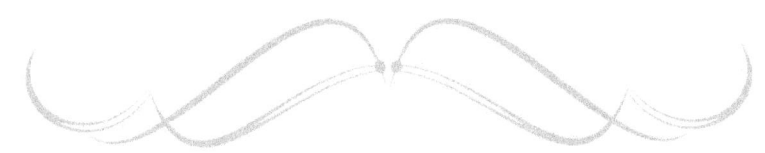

AFTER EARNING HER ACADEMIC DEGREES from Columbia College and the University of Nebraska, Dr. Penny Rafferty Hamilton began her journalism career in 1982.

Later, Penny obtained her private pilot certificate.

In 1991, with her husband, Dr. William Hamilton, they set a world aviation speed record in their own aircraft.

An award-winning writer and photographer, Penny Hamilton is a laureate of the Colorado Aviation, Colorado Women's, and Colorado Authors' Halls of Fame.

Her website is: www.PennyHamilton.com

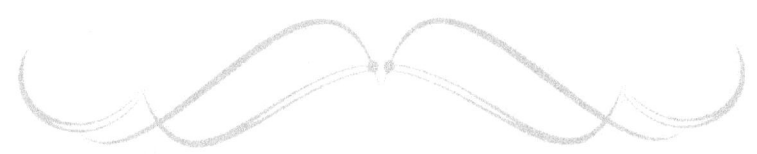

MAIL CALL: THE POWER OF WORDS

Janette Byron Stone

WHILE EACH DRAWN-OUT RING BECKONS a response, her breath holds in all the reasons to hang up. Not well enough.

With a flurry of fumbled jerks, the receiver crashes into its silent place, no longer posing a threat to the tidiness of an ordinary life. The culprit hand jerks back as if it committed a crime.

Despite the physical inertia that wills to dominate, the desire to connect overpowers. She will try again. *This time the phone will ring out. Or. Someone will answer.*

Her finger taps 1. The three-digit area code. Each number a searing step into embers. Smoldering coals lighting the phone face and singeing fingertips. She continues. One number after the other. Done.

The pit of embers trod.

Wait.

The time between the sound of the last number and summons of the first ring takes forever. A summons in whatever language signals the intention of another, known or otherwise, to communicate. Communicate what? A thought? A request? A simple hello? An announcement of joy? A statement of tragedy? A scam? A political hook?

SNAPSHOTS

"Hello." A male voice bearing the monotony of Monday travels through the wire. The time has come to plunge off the cliff of Mt. Silence.

"Is this Steve Hughes?" Anticipating the myriad of possibilities his response could create, doubt and fear sound a warning. It's too late. She has already stepped off.

"It is."

"Were you in Vietnam and did you go to Sydney, Australia for your R and R in June 1969?"

"I did."

"Do you remember meeting someone by the name of Anna Dalton?"

"Anna?" His voice loses ordinary in the recognition of a word. "Is that you?"

Far-away days hurtle into Anna's wife and mother kitchen, erasing the past twenty-five years.

"It is."

"Well, I'll be damned."

Cheap brass spotlights hanging from a freshly painted ceiling focus into a single ray. The telephone receiver becomes a treasure chest. Open the lid to a possibility of good or bad. Keep it sealed and never know.

"I hope you don't mind me calling. I'm writing my master's thesis. I still have your letters, and I'd like to include them. I won't say who they're from or even the dates they were written." *Too garbled.* "And I'd like you to read my proposal." *Too vague.* "Actually, I need your approval. I need to know you're okay with this. You meaning you as representative of the collective whole." *Too quick.*

"Excuse me?"

Clumsy words tumble out of Anna's mouth and break through the wires as a forgotten longing and an immediate

need negotiate hesitant steps in a dance of broken familiarity. Just like the call to another man she didn't know
twenty-years earlier. Her father. Steve was there. *Does
he remember?*

"I met lots of other guys who were on R and R, just
like you." Finding the right words is as hazardous as
walking on hot ashes. "Not exactly just like you. That's
not what I mean," she fumbles. "My cousin went over,
too. You see, I have this collection of over three hundred
letters written from Vietnam, yours included, and I'm
using them to figure out what's important in life. And...
The ethics committee requires permission from the writers
to use your letters. I've had difficulty making contact as
you can imagine. Understandably their addresses have
changed. And, sadly, all too often, I find myself reading
an obituary."

"Can you send it down? Do you have my address?"

"No."

"How did you get my number?"

"I phoned your parents' house. You sent me their details
in the letter you wrote dated December 1969." Her fingers
tangle the off-white coiled phone cord and hold on. "Your
niece answered and told me you were living in Houston.
She asked her dad for your number."

"That would be my brother, Denny. Good thing he and
his family moved into our parents' house after they died."

"I'm sorry they died." She has never met them, but
she's sorry. Their son was little more than a stranger.
And yet there was something. The circumstances of their
meeting. The war. The age they met. The letters. The four
letters he wrote to her surviving all those years. "What
did they die of? When?"

"Old age. Dad ten years ago. Mom, about five now."

Silence.

SNAPSHOTS

There's more to say but whatever it is, or might be, remains hidden in a veil of caution as sometimes happens when the unexpected appears in the moment.

* * *

Today Steve sits opposite Anna in a prairie bar in western Canada, thousands of miles from Sydney and their first meeting. Words, like pinpricks, poke their way into the still air of an afternoon hanging onto summer, seeking to be understood. Or manipulated. Or absorbed.

They grapple with the fact that no matter which way they look at it, what might have been never was. And what never was, will never be.

Nevertheless, the idea tugs like a bad example and invites them to follow. They contemplate the paths they've taken and dare to unravel the past. To wonder what might have happened had the journey been different. Every decision, a choice. One event, over and after another. One word over and after another. One person over and after another. And every choice bound and irretrievably connected to all the others that brought them to this moment.

They dare to ask, but not out loud, what if I'd caught the train instead of the bus? Stayed in bed instead of getting up on any given day? Walked on by instead of stopping to talk? Answered the letter instead of figuring out what to say? Who would be the people weaving color, texture, and form into the fabric of their lives? What tones and shape would they add to the lives of others?

Questions pause in the spaces between them as Steve talks about marrying out of lust rather than love when he returned from Vietnam. About his flashbacks. His treatment at the VA. About his eventual divorce and increasing alienation from his four children. His current affair with Stella.

And as they sit with no answers and nothing more than where they are—at the *Bourbon and Beefsteak* by the fountain on Darlinghurst Road—or the *Texas Tavern* where patrons trampled on peanut shells and shouted above *Creedence Clearwater Revival* rocking the rawness of male energy through the jukebox. Maybe the *Whisky a Gogo* where the sound of Motown yearned for love, cried about loss, and looked to one day while desperate guys and willing girls clung to each other on the undersized parquet dance floor.

"What can I get you guys?"

The waiter's white teeth and brown eyes sparkle down on Steve's brown moustache striped with gray, receding hairline and sinking eyes. His youthfulness is a reminder of how time erodes and corrodes not only the physical but also the emotional and psychological embodiment of who they are as aging humans on their life's journey.

The young man could have been Steve back then. Or any one of them. He also could have been Anna when she waited on tables in the coffee shop with the tireless sparkle of youth and the wide-eyed expectancy of life on the cusp.

"I'd like to try one of your Canadian beers." Steve turns his head with a cautious movement suggesting a stiff neck.

"*Molson* okay?"

"Sure."

"The young waiter turns his smiling eyes to Anna. Patient, as he waits for her to make up her mind.

"Orange juice, thanks."

A light breeze plays with the fringe of the green and beige striped umbrella.

SNAPSHOTS

"Do you remember the day we went to the zoo?" she asks.

"Taronga Park. Every detail. That was quite the storm."

"Yes, it was quite the storm," she echoes. Their eyes meet. The sparkle once translucent replaced with years of experience, now past. If she was single, he might have reached for her hand, or her his, despite the gaping hole of years without contact.

The waiter, an unintentional reminder of the passage of time, places their drinks on the table. His eager, yet comfortable manner suggests he enjoys his job.

"My shout," Anna offers, quick to honor the understanding she and Steve had established on the phone before his arrival. Their reunion cost him the price of a return airfare and her his expenses for the visit.

A breeze sweeps across the deck on its passage west through the small rural town. When the umbrella fringe loses its windy playmate, it settles to a still calm. The heat of the sun steams the brownish bricks of the old building like a sauna.

Steve removes his dark blue, tailored-suit jacket and hangs it, so the sleeves hang evenly down the back of his patio chair. He loosens his tie bearing the insignia of the 173rd Airborne and rolls up the sleeves of his white shirt, so clean it defies the dirt of life.

Anna had difficulty deciding what to wear. In the end she opted for white pants and a pale blue denim shirt—a smart casual look not quite matching his formal suit and tie.

He'd looked like a businessman when he emerged through the arrival doors two hours earlier, carrying a taupe suit bag over his right shoulder. With his left hand in his trouser pocket, he created a picture-perfect magazine image of the guy who'd made it. Military clean and efficient. Young again.

The image would have swept her away in Sydney twenty-five years ago, but this was Edmonton. Twenty-five years later.

"When did you discover you didn't love your wife?"

"Some time in the first year."

"Did she love you?"

"No."

"How do you know?"

"I was low on her list of priorities. There were the kids. Her mother. Her sisters and the rest of the family. Then, there was me."

"Why did you stay together so long?"

"Our first child was on the way when we decided to marry. Then the others kept coming and life carried on."

At five-thirty the *Fieldhouse Stop* fills with workers ready to embrace the end of the work week and the beginning of two days with unpaid freedom.

"Are you ready to meet the family?" she asks, swirling the white straw around the ice cubes in her glass.

"One more beer and I'll be ready," he answers, as the waiter reappears. "So, tell me about Anna."

"Nothing much to tell. I came here, met Dale on a blind date on Valentine's Day, stayed a couple of months, then hopped over to England and Holland to have a look around. Eight months after leaving, I returned to Australia. Dale came to visit. We decided to get married, and we left Australia the next day. We've been here ever since. Just like I told you on the phone."

Steve lifts the brown bottle to his mouth and tips back his head. He's reminded of the twinge in his neck and takes a moment to adjust. "Are you happy?"

"Very."

SNAPSHOTS

"Good." He peels the bottle's label in strips that resemble colorful bacon. His eyes shift to the green plastic table. He nods back and forth processing other possible meanings in Anna's words.

A woman dressed in yellow shorts and a bright floral halter-top sidles by their table on her way to the bar inside. When she speaks, Anna recognizes her as a colleague who never quite became a friend.

"Hi Anna," she says, her eyes on Steve. Her train-tracked brow and widened eyes betray a desperate desire to figure out who the man is sitting opposite Anna.

Steve doesn't seem to notice. "I'm proud of you for writing your thesis."

"Thank you. It was difficult writing about that time, having no-one to consult with who shared those days. I'm glad you were there when I called."

No response.

"I was worried about using the letters. Even though it was my story I was telling, I hoped that if any of you read it, you would consider my work as a tribute. A small contribution to the ongoing healing process around your Vietnam experience. Another thread in the fabric."

Still no response. He again tips the bottle to his mouth. As he lowers it to the table, his fingers and thumb slip around the neck. He circles the bottle until the momentum turns the amber liquid into white froth. He places the bottle back on the table and leans over.

"You know, we don't like to see ourselves as victims. There's been a lot of shit written about our experience over there. Your letters speak for the experience."

"They're not all about war."

"No. They're about kids in war. Being there and trying to stay normal if you know what I mean."

"I believe I understand the writers better now than I did then. I don't think I really got it when I first received the letters. I'm ashamed to say I didn't grasp the intensity of the war back then."

"It's amazing you kept those letters. Moving country and all. How did a girl like you come to be in Kings Cross in the first place?"

"My mother found me a job in a record shop through an old school friend of hers."

"Were all those letters really yours?"

"You read my proposal. My grandma never threw anything out, so they survived." There was a pause. "Did I tell you my cousin, Michael, went over?" The dull roar of a memory abandoned too soon returns.

"What's wrong?"

Anna is lost for words.

"Did he come back?" Steve asks.

Michael has stayed hidden in the recesses of her mind for twenty years. This isn't the time to talk about him.

SNAPSHOTS

Yes, he came back." Butterflies flutter in her chest and the outdoors closet in with a queasy nausea. "Can we talk about something else?"

"Sure."

"Do you remember Carol?"

"Is that the girl who was with you when we met at the fountain? I don't recall her name."

"That was Carol."

"Do you still keep in touch with her?"

"No."

"Nice girl as I recall. But I still want to know who Anna was. Is." He spots the waiter and calls him over.

"Anna was a girl who lived with her mother and sister in her grandmother's house after her father left when she was three."

"You called him."

"At the GPO. You were with me."

"Did you ever meet him?"

"Yes."

"And?"

"And that's how I met Dale. His stepdaughter arranged the blind date. So, there it is. That's Anna." I check my watch. "Dale will have the barbecue ready. He'll be getting anxious."

* * *

That night Anna revisits Steve's question: *Who is Anna?*

Anna, like everyone else, is the product of a certain genetic makeup, her immediate environment, and the choices those combinations allow her to make, not just at critical moments but in the seconds that slip by with every breath.

Over the next few days, the answer to Steve's question rumbles around the inner dungeon of her mind. Some of it she can explain to him on their walks. Some of it she doesn't, can't—the details and the people not yet ready for examination under scrutiny's magnifying glass. The written word would remember.

One of Anna's New Year resolutions in 1967 had been to keep track of day-to-day activities in a diary her grandmother gave her for Christmas. A diary could be as simple as a list of events, or so complex it could rewrite the commandments in the language of her soul. With only a few lines for each entry, her scribbles were limited to half a mousetrap's worth, barely enough to list phone calls and who made them.

As it turned out, it was the letters that opened the memory box, documented, and preserved the experience, set the historical context, and immortalized their writers. Each person, every time he put pen to paper, chiseled the Rosetta Stone of his youth in the script of the soldier, the man, and the friend.

SNAPSHOTS

JANETTE BYRON STONE M.ED. IS one of those restless Aussies who went walk-about as soon as she could. Hungry to know what the rest of the world had to offer, her dream was to teach in different countries and cultures for at least ten years. She had no idea her journey would take her to the Canadian prairie and then to the United States where she and her husband, Tom, now juggle the seasons between tropical Key West and mountainous Idaho.

Passionate about the Arts, she founded and directed award-winning choirs in Australia and Canada and has performed in amateur musicals, professional TV, and film.

Today she satisfies her passion for literary expression by writing books, short stories, newspaper articles, ditties for those who inspire, and the occasional poem. She is most at home writing in the genres of historical fiction and narrative nonfiction.

Drop by for a visit at: www.janettebyronstone.com

SEA STORIES

Valerie Ormond

I'VE ALWAYS LOVED THE SOUND and pulse of the ocean's waves in rhythm with my heart. It makes me feel at home. It shouldn't surprise me, being from proud seafaring roots of Irish, British, and Portuguese folks. Family sea stories include one where my great, great, great Irish grandfather navigated the family home during a storm one night because as a sailor he knew how to read the stars when it was impossible to see through the fog and mist at sea level. And because we are a family who loves the water, including generations of serving different navies, we have our fair share of sea stories.

It was early September 1992, a lovely time of year in Hawaii.

"Come out on the boat with us tomorrow," my friend Brian said, sipping a cold beer at my dining room table on the North Shore of Oahu.

I had been in the Navy for eight years at that point, and I was serving my second tour in Hawaii. I hadn't even asked for one, but it's what they called the needs of the Navy.

My brother chimed in, "Brian's taking me fishing tomorrow before I head back home."

Eddy had been visiting me from Maryland for a month to do some soul and career searching, and it had been a good trip for both of us.

SNAPSHOTS

"You don't even like fishing," I reminded.

Even though he was my big brother by a year, I had to be the sensible one sometimes. He shied away from fishing ever since the kid in Ocean City, Maryland had cast his rod the wrong direction and landed a fishhook in six-year-old Eddy's eyelid. A pretty icky sea story, but I was there, an impressionable five-year-old.

"Okay, fishing is not my favorite, but being out on the ocean in the Hawaiian sunshine doesn't sound so bad." He raised a toast to his newfound buddy, Brian.

I saw my brother happy, which is what he'd been seeking in his visit to Hawaii. If he wanted to spend one of his last days on a high seas adventure, who was I to argue?

I had a twelve-hour watch shift coming up in a few hours. It was the last of a string of watches, so I knew I could sleep afterwards. The expressions, "You can sleep when you're dead", and *carpe diem* (seize the day), took over what should have been my logical response.

Instead, I said, "Tell me when and where, and I'll be there."

Brian said, "Meet us over at the *Waianae Small Boat Marina* when your shift is over. We'll have everything ready—you can just sleep on the bow."

Brian, being a Navy veteran and long-time shift-worker understood what would be on my mind at the end of my upcoming twelve-hour shift.

I dressed in my khaki uniform and left the guys to plan tomorrow's outing. I packed a bag for myself with the essentials—a bathing suit, shorts, tank top, towel, sunscreen, shoes, and sunglasses. I figured Eddy and Brian would take care of everything else while I was working.

I drove across the island of Oahu to the Makalapa compound with a view of Pearl Harbor. Even after being cranky about having to go to work on a Sunday night, the sight of Pearl Harbor and the Arizona Memorial always put emotions in perspective.

I trudged into the Joint Intelligence Center Pacific, standing the seventh night of what were called mid-shifts, or midnight shifts. This one was from 6:00 P.M. to 6:00 A.M. I spent a mind-numbing shift reading intelligence traffic, making connections, and drafting short intelligence reports that I hoped someone would read.

After paying my penance to the Navy that watch, I opened the door out of the windowless building to a glorious sunrise of yellow, orange, and bright blue hues. The geckos chirped as I climbed into my *300 ZX* sports car in my change of clothes, glad I had thrown in a hoodie at the last minute. The air was a tad cool and crisp, but I welcomed the fresh air to chase away thoughts of sleep.

I thought about my brother, and how he'd called me at work one night a few months earlier in the same building I had just left. In distress, he'd been laid off from his job and didn't know where to turn next. I invited him to visit in Hawaii and suggested the aloha spirit might help him find his way, or at least it would be a good escape. He agreed, and after many hours of talking and discovery, he realized he should pursue his passion to be a teacher.

I was glad Eddy had made friends with Brian during the visit because they got along well. And while my brother saw himself as broken at the time due to the unexpected layoff, Brian didn't see him that way. I didn't either, but I was his sister, so it was different.

During that contemplation, I pulled into Waianae harbor on the leeward side of the island and found my companions.

"Ahoy, matey," Brian called from his seventeen-foot powerboat. They had loaded up with supplies—water, beer, chips, lures, bait, and all the fishing gear.

The guys who had enjoyed a full night's sleep radiated with energy preparing the boat for our launch while

SNAPSHOTS

I laid my towel on the bow and took my watch position for the day. I closed my eyes while we pulled out of the harbor on a cloudless day with morning temperatures in the mid-seventies and light trade winds. The purring motor and rocking motion of the small vessel put me to sleep, as it did most Navy sailors.

Pffft....zzzziiinnngggg!

"What was that?" I asked, waking up.

One of Brian's jerry-rigged outrigger poles to hold fishing rods stretched sideways, with the line ripping through it.

"We've got something!" Brian yelled.

Unlike a Navy exercise or operation, we hadn't prepared for this. I scrambled to the aft of the boat where I could do something other than sleep and sunbathe, and Brian turned the driving over to Eddy, while our only skilled fisherman planned what to do next.

Brian watched the rate of the line going out and said, "This is a big one."

"Isn't that the typical fish story?" I joked.

"No, seriously, this is big." Brian's eyes darted from my brother to me. He pulled out a plastic contraption that turned out to be a waist-held fishing rod holder. "I'll show you how to use this. But we'll have to take turns because this fish will wear us out."

That wasn't the best time to remember Eddy was recovering from a hip replacement. Eddy said, "I can drive. Tell me where you want to go."

Brian struggled with the weight pulling hard on the line while he sat in a sturdy chair supporting his outstretched feet on the bulkhead. In flip-flops, of course. The line continued to whiz out at a steady pace without letting up. The sweat dripped down his arms where I could see his veins popping.

Brian barked directions to our new first mate saying things like, "Turn to the leeward, there you go, steady as she goes...not too fast, this line could snap in a second."

I stood by, waiting for my turn, hoping my five-foot-seven frame could handle whatever was on the other end of the line.

The giant fish finally breached out of the water in a show of strength from our opponent. It was a scene from an old Mutual of Omaha commercial with the magnificent dorsal fin and pointed bill in the shape of a rainbow.

We had hooked a big blue marlin, and he wasn't giving up. We screamed with excitement and probably let loose a few obscenities.

I asked Brian, "You ever caught one of these?"

He smiled and answered, "Nope."

"Well, us either, so we're in this together."

Seeing the size of the beast made me want to take my turn even more. Adrenaline pulsed through my veins. Brian had been fighting the big guy for at least an hour at that point and had to be exhausted. Brian didn't only have to contend with his rookie fishing partners but had to continue to shout navigation to my brother.

Now that we'd seen his size, we knew why that giant marlin was taking our seventeen-foot boat for a bit of a ride.

"Okay, let me do my part," I said, moving closer to Brian.

I intently listened while he explained everything I should and should not do. I paid particular attention when he explained the importance of the fishing rod holder and to not let the fish pull me overboard.

The first minutes my heart pumped so hard I didn't realize how much I ached. Bound to do my part, I imitated what I'd seen Brian do by using leverage to provide steady support. But hey, I at least had boat shoes on, so I had an advantage.

Every now and then, there would be a soft let up on the line, and I'd worry that I'd be the one who let the big one get away. My seaborne fighter played a game with me when he would let up and pull harder in this battle for his life.

I kept my station for the second hour while Brian dared to take his eyes off me for a second here and there to give my brother a rest, catch his breath, and take a breather.

"How long will this last?" I asked, and then remembered that was his first marlin.

I'm not sure why I cared, because we weren't about to give up on one of the most exciting events in a sports fisherman's life, and we weren't even sports fishermen. I fought the fatigue of being a human, and the marlin fought the fatigue of fighting the sea. He was giving the humans on the other end of the hook a spectacular fight.

Brian took another turn about the time he probably thought I was either about to let go or to get pulled overboard. I had fought this brave fish with everything I had, amazed at how he impacted every muscle in my body.

"He's starting to let up," Brian said, "but he's still here."

He managed to reel him in while using the boat, tides, and wind direction in his favor at every turn. As he got closer and closer, Brian motioned Eddy to the back of the boat so he could see our catch, which took our breath away.

He was almost illuminated, his silver and blue scales reflecting the Hawaiian sun.

"He's not moving," I said.

"He either died fighting, or he drowned," Brian announced.

I was sad for the fighter, even though I wasn't sure what we would do with the live fish flailing around on board our tiny vessel. He was no longer in stress, and no longer in pain. But I definitely respected that sea creature, and I'll never forget him or his fight.

"Let's get him secured alongside the boat and tow him in," Brian said.

I had flashbacks of Ernest Hemingway's story *The Old Man and the Sea*. "What? Don't you two remember the story *The Old Man and the Sea*?"

Eddy said, "Yeah, I remember the movie where the sharks eat the old man's prize fish."

"Exactly! We can't let that happen."

Exhausted, Brian asked, "What do you want to do?"

I thought about it and ran through options. I remembered the old man in the story, Santiago, made a few bad decisions. I had to make a good one. Then it came to me.

"We'll lasso him."

My shipmates laughed.

"You've got to be kidding me," Eddy said, rolling his eyes. I had always been the horse person, not him.

"We have plenty of sturdy ropes and lines on board, and there are three of us. Sorry, Eddy—don't use your hip." I envisioned it and then continued with my instructions. "One of us will lasso his tail, and the other, his bill. Then we'll pull him aboard."

Brian spoke up, "Have you seen how big he is?"

I looked at the giant fish we pulled alongside and agreed it would be a feat but reminded him. "Yes, but *The Old Man and the Sea*...."

"Let's give it a shot," my brother said. Eddy had his confidence back, and he also had his little sister's back.

SNAPSHOTS

The three of us got into position, and I gave lots of instructions, since my deckhands weren't cowboys. I hadn't done that before either, but at least I had watched enough rodeos to understand the concept of team roping where one ropes the steer's head and the other the back legs. We had a slight edge in that our animal would not be trying to get away from us. We would improvise with the marlin's bill replacing the steer's head and his tail acting as the back legs.

It was preposterous, but no one had a better idea.

We launched into action and after many attempts had the lassos in place with the assistance of our gaff and a fishing net off the side of the boat. With hearts racing and a count of one, two, and three, we hauled Bubba, as Eddy had named him, aboard and out of harm's way.

"We got 'im!" Brian triumphantly shouted.

We shared high fives all around and got a snapshot of the lasso and our rodeo at sea before we headed to shore.

Valerie Ormond with the Marlin and the front lasso over his bill. (Photo by Eddy Ormond)

Once we pulled the boat out of the water, a hoist lifted the fish above us. We posed for photos with our catch of the day that ended up measuring nine feet long and weighing in at more than 300 lbs.

Valerie with the catch of the day. (Photo by Eddy Ormond)

Our dedicated crew had done our part in the conquest and grown as fishing folks throughout the day. We shared memories of a lifetime and a happy ending to our sea story, unlike *The Old Man and the Sea.*

SNAPSHOTS

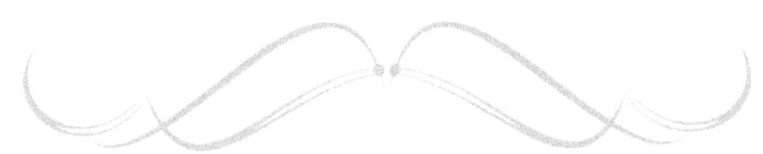

VALERIE ORMOND RETIRED AS A Navy captain after a twenty-five-year career as an intelligence officer, and then founded her own business, *Veteran Writing Services, LLC*. She provides companies professional writing and consulting services and writes and publishes books.

Valerie's three novels, *Believing in Horses*; *Believing in Horses, Too*; and *Believing in Horses out West* have won national and international awards including gold medals in the Military Writers Society of America (MWSA) and first place in the National Federation of Press Women's national communication contest.

Her fiction and non-fiction stories and poems have been published in numerous books, and her articles have appeared in magazines, newspapers, and blogs.

Valerie is the Vice President of MWSA, a previous board member, and a President's Award winner.

She lives in Bowie, Maryland, with her husband Jaime Navarro where they enjoy their family, their three horses, and two dogs.

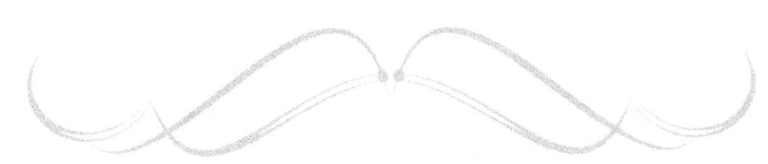

Parris Island

Dwight Jon Zimmerman

*A chapter excerpt from the upcoming novel, **Cursed**.*

"**O**UR FOOTBALL COACH WAS MEAN. AND when I say mean, he was no-nonsense, in-your-face…"

Eric Carter, who had been lost in thought staring out the bus window at the night-shrouded South Carolina countryside, suddenly felt himself jerked around.

"…mean!"

Daniel Patrick Wyndam, sitting in the seat beside him, glared at Eric for a moment, his nose less than an inch from Carter's. Then the powerfully built eighteen-year-old pushed Eric back and laughed, "At least he was to the others."

Wyndam shook his head as he sized up Carter. "The recruiter must have been blind, or desperate, or both to make his quota when he signed you up," he said. "You're skinnier than the water boy we had—and he was a freshman. Why, one of my arms is bigger than one of your thighs."

Eric had to agree, and it wasn't just Wyndam's arms, everything about the six-foot three-inch 230-pound eighteen-year-old screamed "huge".

Wyndam unbuttoned the cuff of his right sleeve and rolled it up. "I figured if you're going to be one of the few and proud, you start by looking the part. I got the muscles thanks to football, so first thing I did after I left the recruiter's office, I went out and got this."

Carter looked down and saw the eagle, anchor, and globe of the Marine Corps tattooed on Wyndam's bicep.

Just then the lights of the Parris Island, South Carolina guard post appeared ahead. The bus carrying the thirty-six recruits, most of them teenagers, a handful in their early twenties, slowed but didn't stop as the Marine guard waved it through.

The bus drove along the two-point-three-mile causeway, past the large sign stating: PARRIS ISLAND: WHERE THE DIFFERENCE BEGINS, where it turned right and, at 1:50 A.M., pulled to a stop by the receiving station.

The driver swung open the door.

Staff Sergeant Wallace Jeffries, in crisp work uniform and wearing a *Smokey the Bear* hat, suddenly appeared before them.

"Now!" the drill instructor shouted. "Sit up straight! Get your eyes on me! If there is anything in your mouth, remove it now!"

Those who were chewing gum or smokeless tobacco immediately did so.

"Now, get off my bus! Let's go! Let's go! Move. Move! MOVE!"

The recruits charged off the bus and stepped onto the yellow footprints arranged four to a row, eighteen rows, painted on the pavement and stood at sort-of attention under the harsh glare of the streetlights.

And so began boot camp for the busload of young men, not all of whom would become members of Platoon 2817.

* * *

Ten weeks later, Recruit Carter lay in his bunk staring up at the dark ceiling. Lights out had happened five minutes ago, but he found himself unable to sleep. He was tired and sore, relieved and, to his surprise, happy and proud.

Two days earlier Platoon 2817 had just completed—survived—the Crucible, an intense fifty-four-hour sleep and food deprivation combat simulation test of knowledge, skills, and teamwork. Next week he was going to graduate and become a marine. No, a *Marine!*

Of the thirty-six recruits who had dashed out of the bus at what now seemed a lifetime ago, nine had washed out, three of them that first night. The first of those three had been Daniel Patrick Wyndam.

Carter shook his head at the memory. Wyndam's troubles had begun as soon as the recruits planted their feet on the yellow footprints painted on the concrete in front of the receiving station.

Sgt. Jeffries, holding his clipboard, took roll call. When he got to Wyndam's name, the drill instructor said, "Recruit WINDam."

Instead of responding with a "here" Wyndam replied, "That's WINEdam, sergeant."

Sgt. Jeffries stopped and then slowly marched toward Wyndam.

When he was exactly six inches from Wyndam's face, the drill instructor roared, "Recruit, if I say your name is Recruit Popeye, your name is Recruit Popeye. If I say your name is Recruit Simple Simon, it's Recruit Simple Simon. And if I say your name is Recruit... Little... Bo... Peep... It's RECRUIT LITTLE BO PEEP! Is that understood, Recruit Little Bo Peep?"

The stunned Wyndam croaked a barely audible, "Yes, sir."

SNAPSHOTS

That earned him another round of chewing out and only after the fourth time did Wyndam manage to shout a response loud enough to satisfy the sergeant, or at least cause him to stop.

They were then led into recruit station for processing.

Wyndam's breaking moment happened when they were inventorying their civilian clothes and affects. They were in the transition period between doffing civilian attire and receiving the assorted military clothing they'd need. During that transition, the recruits wore nothing but T-shirts and briefs.

Though some of the recruits sported tattoos, Wyndam's was the only one featuring the Marine Corps emblem. When Sgt. Jeffries saw it, it was as if a red flag had been waved before a bull. Before anyone realized what was amiss, the sergeant was in the recruit's face again.

In a low voice dripping with menace, Jeffries pointed to the tattooed bicep, and asked, "What is that?"

"It's my Marine Corps tattoo, ser—"

Jeffries cut him off with a sneer. "My? MY? There is no 'my' in your vocabulary, Recruit Little Bo Peep. You are a recruit. You have done nothing to earn the title Marine. You wearing that tattoo is an insult to MY Marine Corps. And you will pay starting now by doing push-ups Recruit Little Bo Peep. When in the up position you will say, 'I am a recruit.' At the down position, you will say, 'I am not a Marine.' And you will continue until I tell you to stop. Now drop down and begin."

By that time, the recruits had been up for more than twenty hours, tired and disoriented by the incessant and frenetic chivvying by Jeffries and other drill instructors— the beginning of the basic training indoctrination. The ashen-faced Wyndam promptly got into position on the deck (they had already learned that it wasn't a "floor").

Upon reaching the full "up" position, he said, "I am a recruit." Upon reaching the full "down" position, he said, "I am not a Marine."

Nine times Wyndam repeated the cycle. Then, as he was about to begin the tenth, Wyndam suddenly burst into tears.

"It's not fair! I don't deserve this chickenshit!" he wailed, collapsing onto the deck.

Jeffries grabbed one of Wyndam's arms, picked up the trembling soon to be former Marine recruit, and quickly escorted him into another room and out of Platoon 2817.

Eric knew he should go to sleep, but his mind kept bouncing from one memory to another: rolling around half-naked in the large sandbox called the Pit, getting eaten alive by the chiggers—sand fleas—and then putting back on his utilities uniform.

Recruit Kelly O'Casey, the platoon klutz and his repeated off-key singing of *The Marine Corps Hymn* after losing his grip on the obstacle course rope climb and falling into the water-filled pit, because he always lost his grip on the rope climb... more chiggers... vomiting after getting a lungful of tear gas in the "gas chamber" test experience... still more chiggers... the morning three-mile runs with the double-time last effort... even more chiggers...

Firing week with the rifles and earning the Expert Sharpshooter Badge (already he was thinking about applying to be a sniper) and always... chiggers.

So many of the memories blurred into each other, but two incidents stood out with singular clarity. The first occurred when they put into practice their budding combat skills in "Warrior Week".

It happened on one of the nights they crawled through a patch of woods, booby-trapped with flares—part of their

SNAPSHOTS

Principles of Night Movement training. The object was for the recruits to crawl along booby-trapped paths and reach their drill instructors without tripping any of the flare booby traps.

Of the fifteen flare grenade traps, the platoon managed to trip only four, a low score that pleased the drill instructors. Carter didn't trip any, which he thought was a surprise because at one point early along his path he saw something that scared the hell out of him.

O'Casey (of course) had tripped the first flare. Carter froze, burying his face in the crook of his elbow to retain his night vision.

When the flare extinguished, Eric lifted his head—and found himself looking at a wolf less than thirty feet away, watching him.

Carter froze, the hairs on the back of his neck stiffened. He blinked and shook his head in disbelief. When he looked back, the wolf was gone.

It had happened so quickly Carter wondered if he had truly seen it. But, the image of the wolf's face and its piercing blue eyes was indelibly stamped in his memory.

Just before lights out the following day, Carter couldn't contain himself any longer. He marched (such was the indoctrination training that he didn't think to walk) over to the barracks' drill instructor's quarters and knocked on the door.

"Come in, recruit," said the voice inside.

Carter entered, closed the door behind him, stood at attention and said, "Recruit Carter requests permission to ask a question, sir."

Gunnery Sergeant Roger Mathews, a member of the three-man drill instructor team responsible for 2817, was on duty that night. He looked up from his desk and said, "What's your question, Recruit Carter?"

He paused as he nervously framed what to say. "Sergeant Mathews... while crawling on the path during the recent Principles of Night Movement exercise, this recruit... is believed to have seen... a wolf. Are there wolves on Parris Island, Sergeant Mathews?"

A silence as thick as the humid South Carolina night suddenly filled the air-conditioned room.

Sergeant Mathews got up from behind his desk and slowly strode over to Carter until his face was inches from the recruit's. With his eyes locked onto those of Carter's, the drill instructor said in a voice so low it was almost a whisper, "Your eyes played a trick on you, Recruit Carter—caused by the flickering light of the flares hitting the vegetation. The only wolves on Parris Island have two legs—and they're Marines. Now drop down and give me twenty."

Recruit Carter immediately went to the deck, did twenty quick push-ups, and silently returned to his bunk.

SNAPSHOTS

The second incident occurred on the last day of the Crucible, in the pre-dawn hours of the final morning. The exhausted recruits had just gotten into formation for a last, forced march.

Out of the woods suddenly emerged three Marine Corps officers, two lieutenants flanking a colonel.

The contrast between the recruits' Marine Corps Combat Utility Uniforms that were wet, dirty, reeking of rotting vegetation and body odor, and the crisp, clean MCCUUs of the officers could not have been starker. But what stood out most to the recruits was that the colonel was blonde, female, and looked like she could have walked off a *Sports Illustrated* swimsuit issue photo shoot.

"Atten-SHUN!" shouted Gunnery Sergeant Mathews, snapping a salute.

"At ease, sergeant," said the colonel, returning the salute. "As you were briefed, this inspection won't take long."

"Yes, ma'am," he replied, falling in to escort the colonel while the lieutenants, both holding computer tablets, took up position two steps back.

The group proceeded to slowly walk down the formation, the colonel looking into the face of each grimy, sweaty recruit she passed. She then stopped in front of one recruit.

Sergeant Mathews immediately said, "This is Recruit Gregory Wilson, colonel."

"Thank you, sergeant," the colonel replied, her nostrils momentarily flaring. Then, with a slight smile she said, "Yes... He smells right."

The lieutenants' fingers immediately played over the touch screens of their tablets, making notations as the colonel resumed walking. Carter was the last person in the front row.

When the colonel got to him, she again stopped, her hypnotic blue eyes gazed deeply into his.

Carter knew he had never seen her before, but despite his exhaustion, he sensed that there was something familiar in her gaze.

"Recruit Eric Carter, ma'am," said Mathews.

"Yes," the colonel said, in a half-whisper. "The one who smells... interesting."

Then turning to face Mathews, she briskly said, "Thank you, sergeant, we have finished. Our apologies for the interruption of Platoon 2817's training, but it was necessary. You may carry on."

"Yes, colonel." replied Mathews, saluting. As the officer trio marched away, the drill instructor shouted, "Two eight one seven, left face. On the double. March!"

* * *

Staring up at the blank ceiling of Platoon 2817's barracks, Carter again mentally asked himself, *What the hell was that all about?*

His brow furrowed as a thought suddenly struck him. Though it was dark when the officers did their inspection of the platoon, Carter recalled seeing one unusual thing about their uniforms—none of the officers wore name tags.

Then a flash of recognition hit him, and he involuntarily shuddered at the memory. The look in the colonel's eyes and their color. They were the same as those of the wolf he saw that night during Warrior Week.

He sighed and shook his head. Then he rolled over and went to sleep.

Meanwhile, three bunks away, Gregory Wilson was reviewing his own thoughts and questions about the colonel.

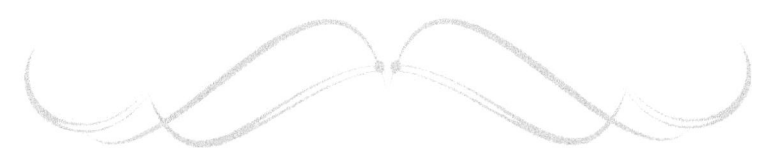

DWIGHT JON ZIMMERMAN IS AN award-winning #1 New York Times bestselling author. In a career spanning more than forty years in the publishing industry he has written everything from comic books (for *Marvel Comics* and *DC Comics*) to hundreds of military history articles and more than two dozen books.

His book *First Command*, about the first commands of famous generals, was an award-winning documentary aired on the *Military Channel*. He co-authored *Uncommon Valor; The Medal of Honor and the Warriors Who Earned It in Afghanistan and Iraq* which won the Military Writer Society's Founder's Award, the organization's highest honor, and was the first book to contain the complete history of the Medal of Honor.

A former president of the Military Writers Society of America, he lives in Brooklyn, NY.

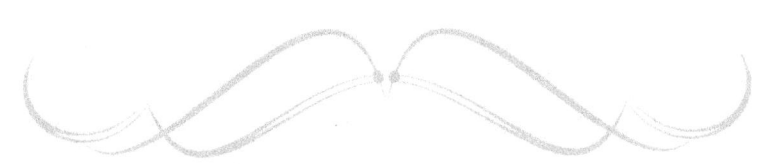

CHERRY JUMP

Joe Epley

RUDY STRUTTED AS HE PROUDLY wore the shiny silver wings of a new paratrooper. At nineteen, he had completed three weeks of push-ups, running, PT, constant yelling by instructors, and five parachute jumps. It was worth all the pain to be a member of the greatest brotherhood on earth—an airborne soldier.

His ego was deflated, however, when he reported to his first assignment after jump school.

Rudy was welcomed to Company B, 2nd Battalion, 508th Parachute Infantry, 82nd Airborne Division by First Sergeant Tony Johnson, who roared, "You are in the first platoon, PFC Cherry, but you have latrine detail with the other cherries in the company."

Cherries were qualified paratroopers who had not yet jumped with an airborne line unit.

The following morning, Rudy learned his cherry jump would be that evening. He tried to look cool and mask his excitement when the first sergeant told him, "PFC Cherry. You're number one in the door."

Leading paratroopers out of the airplane is an honor most airborne soldiers cherish. Rudy wasn't afraid of jumping, but he was petrified of falling out the door before he was supposed to leap. The first man, according to training protocol, stood in the door for nearly a minute, hands outside the plane, flat against the fuselage, not holding to anything.

In Rudy's mind, nothing could be more embarrassing than falling from the plane before getting the "go" command.

Rudy's aircraft was an old C-119, a flying boxcar that belonged to an Air Force reserve unit. In addition to being noisy, it was slow, bumpy, and in 1965, obsolete.

As he rode to Pope Air Force Base, Rudy was sick from worrying about having to stand in the door for a full minute. He did his best to show bravado, but the other men knew he was a cherry. No insignia showed his amateur status, but the other soldiers took glee in making fun of the cherries.

First Sergeant Johnson led the company through the safety drills that precede every airborne operation. As jumpmaster, he was responsible for the lives of all personnel jumping from the C-119.

As he had done hundreds of times before, after he had donned his parachute and reserve, Johnson personally inspected each man. He made certain there was no twist in the webbing or other malfunctions in the parachute harness. The jumpmaster made sure the quick release was locked and the safety pin inserted, the forty-pound T-10 parachute was securely hooked to his harness, and the reserve parachute was properly attached over his belly.

Ending the inspection, Johnson took the end of the static line that automatically pulled opened the main parachute when he exited the aircraft and handed it to Rudy. Rudy draped the snap link over his shoulder and fastened it to his reserve carrying handle. That made it easy to reach when he had to hook himself to the anchor line cable.

All simple procedures but deadly if not precisely followed.

Forty-six paratroops boarded the C-119 and waddled to canvas-webbed seats. Rudy led the starboard stick and sat beside the open jump door at the rear of the plane. The jumpmaster sat across the aircraft from him, next to the opposite door, which was also open.

After what seem like an hour of the C-119 pilots revving up twin *Pratt & Whitney* engines, the flying boxcar taxied for takeoff.

The flight was forty-five minutes, out over the vast pine forests surrounding Camp Mackall west of Fort Bragg and then back to Holland drop zone where the men would jump.

"A milk run," said the Air Force loadmaster, who didn't bother to close the two jump doors. He, too, wore an emergency chute.

Looking through the open door, Rudy was mesmerized by the ground rushing by 5,000 feet below.

Please Lord, don't let me fall out before I have to jump, he silently prayed.

Sergeant Johnson stood up, appearing as if he might fall out but he remained steady as he yanked on the anchor line cables to make sure the metal wires were securely fastened.

He hooked his static line, grabbed the door edges, and hung his head outside to see if any obstacles existed. Satisfied nothing would interfere with his jumpers, he conversed through the noise with the loadmaster.

Signaling to the passengers in the airplane, the jumpmaster held his hands out in front, five fingers extended on one hand and one on the other, and shouted, "Six minutes!"

Following was the one-minute warning.

The airplane gradually dropped to one-thousand feet and slowed to 130 knots, the jump altitude and speed.

SNAPSHOTS

After checking again outside the plane, the sergeant yelled, "Get Readyyyy!"

I'm going to do it, Rudy thought.

"Stand up!" the jumpmaster yelled as he raised his hands in an upward motion.

Forty-six soldiers, including Rudy, struggled to their feet.

Outside the aircraft, a civilian *Cessna 180*, out for a casual joy ride, unexpectantly rose in front of the C-119, shocking the Air Force pilot and causing him to sharply veer to avoid a mid-air collision.

As the violent maneuver took place, Rudy lost his balance and fell forward into the gap and the void beyond.

First Sergeant Johnson and the loadmaster tried to maintain their balances as the aircraft lurched. They watched in horror as Rudy fell toward the open threshold.

Both reached for the falling man but failed.

As Rudy slipped out the door, eyes wide with panic, he tried to grab the airplane, but touched only air. He didn't see his would-be rescuers. In his hand, he held a useless static line.

The roar of the aircraft ceased as the C-119 disappeared from Rudy's unbelieving eyes. Trees rushed up to meet him.

Training kicked in, and he pulled the D-ring on his reserve parachute.

The canopy popped out 400 feet above the ground and slowed his descent. The main T-10 parachute was still in the tray on his back, a useless cargo.

Falling, Rudy recalled lessons drilled into him from jump school.

"When landing in trees, keep your legs together, fold your arms over you face and duck you head to the crook of your arms."

He quickly folded his arms and pushed his legs together as he plunged through the top of a tall loblolly pine.

He heard the smashing of body and crackling of limbs and felt something pop in his leg.

The canopy draped over the tree top as he crashed through the branches and jerked to an abrupt halt. He dangled twenty-five feet above the ground.

In the C-119, Sergeant Johnson hung his head outside the door trying to spot the falling soldier. Relief at seeing the white canopy open below, he crawled back inside and jerked the communication link from the loadmaster.

He shouted, "Pilot, this is the jumpmaster. We lost one of our men. He fell out of the plane without hooking up. I saw his emergency chute open. We have several men still on the deck, maybe hurt, from those aerobatics you pulled. I am aborting the jump. Fly us back to Pope."

The pilot relayed information to Pope Air Force Base about the missing jumper and the *Cessna*, which now was out of sight—its pilot cursing the Air Force for nearly running him down.

Rudy hung from a tall pine, paralyzed with fear and the pain of a broken leg. It took more than two hours for rescuers to find him. Hanging in agony, his cries for help seemingly unheard.

* * *

A soldier climbed the tree and helped Rudy, who was suspended only four feet away, swing over to the trunk. It was a painful but successful maneuver.

After tying the injured man securely to the trunk, a rope was rigged to the tree before being tied to the jumper's harness. The suspension lines that precariously held him to the swaying tree were cut away, and Rudy was gently and safely lowered to medics and a stretcher.

EMTs rushed to stabilize the broken leg, while an officer slapped Rudy's shoulder and cheerfully said, "Hell of a way to make a cherry jump."

* * *

Rudy's broken leg took three months to heal. He drew jump pay during that time, but only had light duty. There were investigations by the company, battalion and brigade commanders to make sure he didn't leave the airplane on purpose. The final conclusion was Rudy's fall was an accident. The first sergeant kept reminding the young soldier, however, that Rudy was still a cherry.

"Falling out of the plane without hooking up doesn't count in this man's army."

In late April 1965, Rudy was cleared to jump again just as his battalion received orders to participate in Operation Power Pack. Communist fighters threatened the government of Dominican Republic. No time for a practice jump. He joined his company in full combat gear, weapons, live ammunition, and parachutes as they loaded C-130s for a long flight to war in the Caribbean nation.

The troops didn't know what awaited them, but he didn't care. He was going to get his cherry jump into a combat zone.

Half-way to the Dominican Republic, his fitful sleep was interrupted by the intercom on the flight informed the paratroopers that, "the runway in Santo Domingo was safe."

The planes would land and the troops deploy on the airport. "There will be no jump."

Rudy and the paratrooper's ego sagged. But he was going into combat.

With rifles at the ready, the troops ran from the C-130 and set up security around the plane before it cut its engines. But no enemy was at the airport. There were a few sniper shots in the days following their arrival, enough to earn the combat infantry badge.

It was over a month before the division started proficiency jumps and Rudy finally got his cherry jump—a Hollywood leap into a sugar cane field.

By the time his battalion was back at Fort Bragg, Rudy was considered a combat veteran although never shot at nor fired his weapon at an enemy. His company served hundreds of meals, distributed water, and provided security to thousands on both sides of the conflict.

The government was stable. By the end of his tour, he had made six proficiency jumps in the Dominican Republic but none as first man in the door or as exciting as that first experience with the 82nd Airborne.

SNAPSHOTS

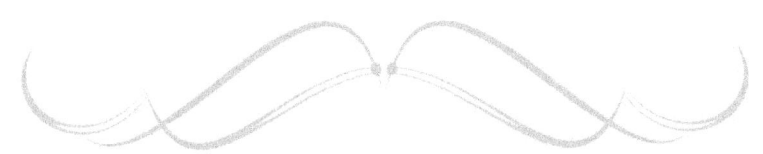

J OE EPLEY RETIRED FROM THE Army Reserve as a master sergeant and a master parachutist. He served over fourteen years in the Army's Green Berets.

His newest novel, *A Passel of Trouble; The Saga of Loyalist Partisan David Fanning* is available online. His first book, *A Passel of Hate*, received a silver medal from the Military Writers Society of America and was named, "Editor's Choice" by the Historical Novel Society.

Joe is a member of the Halls of Fame at the UNC School of Journalism and the Defense Information School. His successes also earned him the state of North Carolina's prestigious *Order of the Long Leaf Pine*.

After heading his own public relations firm in Charlotte and Raleigh, N.C., Joe retired for good in Greenville, S.C.

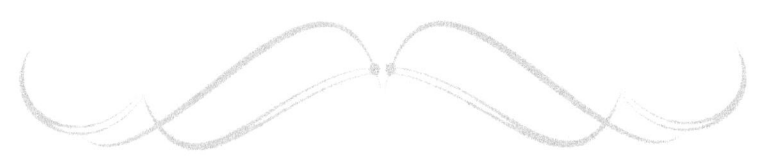

THE IDITAROD: DOGS BARKING, TAILS WAGGING

Bruce Thomas

One thousand and forty-nine miles. Over snow and ice.

To the "Distant Place". The Iditarod sled dog race moves.

The temperature is always cold with the wind blowing.

But this is no ordinary race. The athletes are notable.

The dogs bark and wag their tails in Willow,

They bark and wag their tails in Skwentna,

They pull their sleds and mushers past Ophir and Galena

The tails never stop. The barking shows their eagerness to pull.

The men and women behind the sleds

Talk of their athletes. Of their friends. Of their partners.

The teams care and nurturing are vital,

Humans never sleep or eat first. The dogs are always first.

The sleds move behind the dogs' tails.

SNAPSHOTS

The weight is pulling against the harness.

The sleeping bags, the food, the snowshoes and the ax.

The musher runs, pushes, and hides from the weather.

The dogs lean into the wind.

Crossing the ice while the gusts spear their eyes and fur.

The mushers yell commands and speak encouragement,

Because these pets are much more than extras in this journey

They are the mission, the reason the race is waged.

Joe Reddington, Dorothy Page, and others

Saw the dogs were being phased out. They were being replaced.

Alaska was changing due to snow machines and airplanes.

They wanted to hear the barks and watch the tails wagging.

In 1973 the path of historical significance was followed.

Out over the Alaskan wilderness, the dogs pulled forward.

Help isn't provided during this first trek, but Nome awaits.

Feeling spoiled, we can watch from our computers in the warmth

Of our homes. As the dogs' breathing steams, the paws grab the ground.

The chute awaits. Will they endure the sea ice this year?

The dogs bark. The tails wag. The musher's sleep is restricted.

Standing with their lights probing the night. Where is the trail?

The race goes on. We are restoring the Serum Run of 1925.

The Iditarod sled dog race endures,

The natives make their sandwiches and bake their pies,

The checkpoints come alive with straws, barks, and snacks.

At checkpoints, the mushers sign in on a clipboard,

While many slackers watch on the internet.

What is the reason for the race?

It is the dogs. The barks. The tails.

And at times, occasionally, the mushers.

Names like Butcher, Mackey, Seavey, and Swenson.

But the actual names we should remember are

The ones who have pulled for all of the miles.

Barking and wagging. Sleeping and eating.

Running and trotting. Pulling and pulling.

Granite, Balto, Togo, Tolstoy, and Andy

These are the names we should remember.

Because this Great Race is about one thing,

It is about the DOGS.

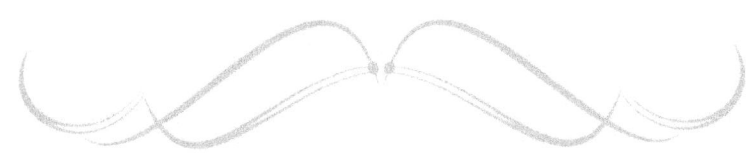

B RUCE THOMAS IS A GRANDPA, screenplay writer, and freelance author. A retired US Air Force fighter pilot, and a former commercial airline captain, he has two fictional mystery/thriller books published.

The Hope of the South (2019) and *Chaos Above the Sand* (2021) are in his *Special Projects Unit* series.

He lives in Overland Park, Kansas with his wife, Vivian.

See more at: www.BruceThomasAuthor.com

The Bottom Line

Annette Langlois Grunseth

Not far from boyhood he was sent to war,
deployed to a valley in the shadow of death—
chaos in the jungle, the agony it bore,
the blood, dust, and smells stole his breath.

Viet Cong attacked from tunnels underground
in chaos of ambush, he was ordered to kill.
Snipers in the trees fired hundreds of rounds,
both sides were shooting when his buddy went still.

Death was so quick, it shocked right to his core,
when he came back home, that scene flooded back,
nightmares of trauma bled deep grief and gore.

He was never the same, still living the attack
then cancer from war seized him cell by cell,
dying, he asked, "Do soldiers go to hell?"

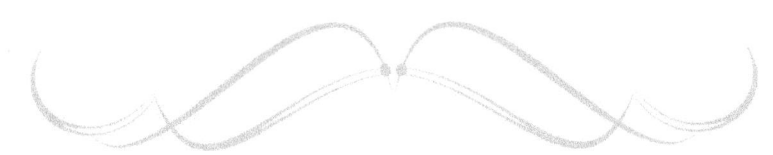

ANNETTE LANGLOIS GRUNSETH, GREEN BAY, WI, is retired from a career in marketing and public relations. She is the author of two books, received the 2022 Hal Prize for poetry, a 2022 gold medal from the Military Writers Society of America for *Combat and Campus: Writing Through War*, and received a Pushcart prize nomination with her book *Becoming Trans-Parent: One Family's Journey of Gender Transition*.

She has been published in *Wisconsin People & Ideas, Bramble, The Poeming Pigeon, Soundings: Door County in Poetry,* and *Halfway to the North Pole*. She has received awards from the Wisconsin Fellowship of Poets, Wisconsin Academy, The Mill, A Place for Writers. She is a member of MWSA, Write On Door County, and Wisconsin Fellowship of Poets.

In her free time, she enjoys bicycle trails, kayaking, and camping in state and national parks.

Learn more at: annettegrunseth.com

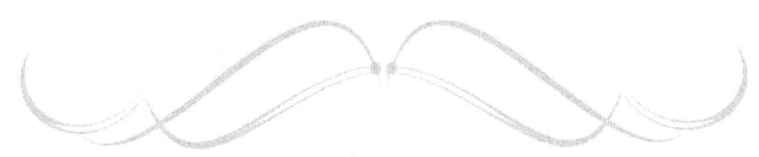

As Law is to Justice

Paul D. Burgess

"Ski" York painted dope on the linen tail of a Soviet trainer while a Russian performed the same task on the ailerons. The cavernous hangar doors had been rolled open that morning to light the interior. Needles of tepid daylight stabbed between the wall planks of the crude structure, seemingly built out of green lumber and apathy. Outside squatted several trainers, faded and mud-spattered. Beyond them, under a lead-gray sky, stretched the bleak and barren plain that constituted the airfield.

Toward the back, Emmens and Herndon repaired an inner tube while Pohl pushed a broom and Laban, along with several other Russians, unloaded boxes from a small truck. All mindless work, but it made the days go by a little faster. York was grateful for a job that kept him around airplanes even if he was never allowed to fly them.

Mikhail, their government minder, aimlessly milled among the mechanics, the aircraft, and the Americans in his charge. A nice enough kid—young, earnest, and doubtless chosen for his English skills and not his socialist zeal. He had been in the role ever since the five Americans were forced onto the train in Vladivostock months earlier. Moscow could have assigned a commissar to the role. Mercifully, they settled on Mikhail.

SNAPSHOTS

Having no wristwatch, Mikhail surmised the time, whistled loudly, and minutes later the six of them were slogging down the village's muddy street—less a street than an open area amidst a collection of unpainted dwellings randomly positioned without any sign of civic planning.

Upon first seeing their new home, York and his crew agreed it looked like the set of a cowboy movie but with camels and donkeys instead of horses, and turbans and skull caps instead of ten-gallon hats. No saloons, of course, in that part of the Soviet Union's southern empire. But the village did have one thing to which no movie could do justice—the stench of raw sewage.

They headed toward the open-air market, sidestepping overloaded donkeys being switched along by their drivers.

"Christ, that's an ugly horse," Herndon said of the camel tied to a wooden rail. The joke used to be funny. The animal growled, raised its tail, and dropped a load of manure, which slapped onto the mud.

"I buy food. You wait here," Mikhail said, and he headed into the warren of food stands, their proprietors using horsehair whisks to sweep the flies from their meager stock.

In broken English, one of the vendors called to Emmens, who approached him with friendly familiarity. The other Americans milled among the tables, idly examining their meager offerings—a tiny pyramid of stunted apples here, a few turnips there.

Mikhail returned, bundle in hand, and they resumed their amble up the street toward the cottage.

York brought up the rear and Emmens sidled close.

"Abdul says any time we want," he whispered.

"I told you to forget it, Bob."

"He can't take his eyes off your ring. He says it would pay for everything."

"I said forget it."

"I just can't figure you, Ski."

"We have our orders."

"To sit out the war in this shit hole? What kind of order is that?"

"The lawful kind. The only kind that matters."

"Ya know, Ski, for a West Pointer, you sure—"

Again, York stopped to face Emmens. The West Point reference was too much.

"You're damned right I'm a West Pointer—the only one on the mission, I might add. I bleed army green, so watch your footing, lieutenant."

York struggled to keep his anger in check. It wasn't so much anger as impatience, frustration, weariness. And none of it was directed at his co-pilot, but rather at their predicament. It ate him up—was eating him alive—that his nation was at war, a war they were losing, last he had heard. It ate him up that everyone who knew anything knew it was a war that would be decided in the air. It ate him up that he and his trained crew were to spend the war's duration in that Stalinist backwater.

He took a breath and put a hand on Emmens's shoulder.

"Look, Bob, I don't like this set-up any more than you do. We're all agreed that it stinks. You keep talking about this ring." York held it close to Emmens' face. "See that motto? DUTY, HONOR, COUNTRY. The first word is duty. As commander of this crew, I received my orders directly from Ambassador Standley, with Colonel Yeaton, his air attache, sitting right there to put General Arnold's imprimatur on the whole stinking deal. We are to submit to Moscow's internment order. We are not to attempt any escapes. We are to cooperate in every particular. Those are our orders, and I always follow my orders. Understood?" York turned and resumed the march up the road.

SNAPSHOTS

Their quarters, a lone cottage surrounded by a high wall, stood forlorn just outside the village's perimeter. Behind the back wall snaked a long road, disappearing into the horizons in both directions. Mikhail closed the gate behind them.

Inside, the cottage was small and spartan. Mikhail took his package into the kitchen to prepare dinner. The Americans dropped into the rustic chairs and cots lining the walls.

York opened the front door and stood on the threshold. He leaned against the jamb and took in the scene. A column of men approached down the road. He watched them for several moments.

"Hey, Mike," he called over his shoulder. "There's a column of guys coming down the road."

In the kitchen, Mikhail chopped a cabbage. "Soldiers?"

"Don't look like it."

"Please shut door until they pass."

The column drew nearer. It was small, a couple dozen men in all. An armed guard led at its head with another at the tail. The column's front half disappeared from view behind the high garden wall, and the back half, still visible, halted. The men dropped wearily to the ground—obviously a rest break.

York started to close the door but caught himself. One of the men said something. York listened briefly, then shut the door.

Across the cottage's interior and through the door into the kitchen, York spotted Mikhail standing at the open kitchen window chopping cabbage for the evening meal. He gathered the green mound in both hands and dropped it into the large pot sitting atop the wood-burning stove. Unwrapping the meat from its greasy newsprint, he commenced on it with the knife. White with fat, it was too small to feed six men even before it rendered down to half its size in the large iron pan.

York stepped casually through the cottage and out the back door into the overgrown garden. Stepping over the construction debris from past repair projects—roofing tiles, broken window glass—he turned one of a pair of wooden, high-backed garden chairs to face the garden wall, which climbed high above the tangle of bushes and vines at its base. Then he lit up a cigarette and waited.

The kitchen window looked out into the garden. It framed Mikhail, who had his head down, still focused on his cutting board. The bite of the local cigarette was foul—it had to have been made with camel manure. Mikhail raised his head and looked at York, who offered a friendly wave. *Good.*

York sat down, disappearing from Mikhail's view behind the chair's high back. Fishing on the ground, he found a shard of window glass, swept the mud from it with his thumb, and discreetly searched its reflection for the kitchen window and Mikhail. Mikhail turned and disappeared. He would have been taking the meat to the pan.

York moved quickly. He wedged his burning cigarette between the planks of the chair's high back and scrambled on hands and knees into the bushes at the wall's base. He followed the wall, searching.

Emmens and Herndon had reported a small breach in the wall on one of their clandestine explorations of the property—the first attempt in a seemingly endless and borderline insubordinate series of escape plans.

About three yards along he came upon it, a gap of about six inches in width and eight to ten inches high. Large patches of the wall's lime-washed plaster had fallen away revealing the river stones beneath. A discarded length of pipe nearby indicated past efforts to enlarge the aperture by prying free some of the smaller stones.

SNAPSHOTS

York put his face to the ground. Through the hole, he could see ragged clothing on one side and the hand of another man on the other.

In Polish, he whispered through the hole.

"Any Poles out there? I heard someone speaking Polish."

There was an initial silence, then a whispered reply, "Who are you?"

"Edward York. Captain, US Army Air Corps."

"You are an American? Yet you speak Polish?"

"I was born in Poland. We moved to America when I was a baby. My family name is Cichowski."

"Hey, there's an American here," the voice discreetly said to his companions. "On the other side of the wall. He speaks Polish."

A barely audible exchange ensued among the prisoners as the word was passed.

"Your name is York now?"

"Yes. I thought it would make it easier to get into West Point if I had a more American name."

"Your father was not offended at this?"

"It was his idea. Who are you? Where are you going?"

Now a second voice entered the conversation. It belonged to the owner of the hand York was looking at. The man went to one elbow, though still no faces were visible. This second voice spoke faster. A bit louder, more high-strung.

"Air corps. You are a pilot?"

"Yes."

"We have heard rumors of Polish flyers fighting for England. Have you heard such rumors?"

"I only know what I read in the papers. The Germans tried to destroy Britain's air force so they could invade.

There was an air battle over England. They're calling it the Battle of Britain."

"Who won?" asked the first Pole.

"The British, but just barely."

"And there were Poles who flew with the British in this battle?" asked the second Pole.

"Many. Several squadrons."

York perceived quiet weeping.

"I told you, Pavel," he said between sobs. "I told you. I pray to God to take me now. It is unbearable."

"Pull yourself together, Dominic," Pavel said flatly. "You'll get your wish soon enough."

"What's his problem?"

No answer.

York allowed the one called Dominic a moment to regain his composure. "You guys are pilots too?"

"Some of us. Me and Dominic. A few others farther down the line. The rest of us are infantry officers. A few cavalry and artillery officers."

"You sure your friend's okay?"

"Why are you here, Cichowski?"

"We've been interned for the duration of the war. My crew and me. That's all I can tell you. Why are you here?"

"We are the last of Poland's officer corps."

"Where are the rest? Prison camps somewhere?"

"Dead. All dead. Executed in the Katyn Forest," answered Dominic, his response punctuated with sniffs and gasps. "The flower of Poland. Shot and buried in the Katyn Forrest."

A moment passed as York absorbed the answer.

"I've never heard of Katyn Forest. The Germans did this?"

SNAPSHOTS

"No. The Russians," Pavel answered. "The Germans invaded from the west three years ago, and the Russians from the east. The Polish army surrendered to the Russians. The officers were separated out. Everyone, from subaltern to field marshal, was taken to the Katyn Forest and shot. Thousands and thousands. Shot."

"How did you guys survive?"

Dominic, now composed, answered. "About eight hundred of us were diverted from the rest as a work party before the massacres. We heard about them from some German prisoners. They discovered the bodies before they were captured."

A noise caught York's attention. In the yard.

"Wait! Shh!"

York gently pushed some vegetation aside to see Mikhail step into the yard with a cooking pot, which he placed under a pump spigot and proceeded to fill with water. At the chair, York's cigarette continued to generate its rising curls of smoke, and Mikhail perceived nothing amiss. He carried the pot back into the kitchen.

York continued. "You guys are pretty lucky, I'd say."

"Lucky?" Dominic chuckled dryly. "We lost our war. Our comrades were murdered. And now we die in the service of their murderers. We are thrice damned."

"How many of you are left?"

"Of eight hundred in the work detail, we now number about thirty," replied Pavel.

"What do you do? Where are you going?"

"We clear minefields. If there is time, we do it on hands and knees prodding the earth with sharp sticks," said Dominic. "If there is no time, the Russians herd us through them like goats. They shoot the laggards with scoped rifles."

"Jesus." The mental image was a lot to process. "Why don't you try to escape?"

"To where?" Pavel responded.

"Escape?" Dominic said a bit too loudly. He was becoming emotional again. "We pine for death as you pine for home."

"Then why not go take a poke at one of your guards? I'm sure he'd be happy to put a bullet through your head."

"Because that would be suicide," said Dominic. "It is against the laws of God and the Holy Catholic Church. So, we wait. For peace and the final justice of death."

"Law and justice aren't always the same thing, are they?" York offered. He immediately regretted the insensitivity for, though he might have gratified himself with his insight, it was coldly useless to the doomed men invisible on the other side of the wall.

Dominic paused. "No."

"Why didn't you try to get out with the other pilots? The ones flying for the British?"

"Because we were ordered not to." Dominic, again too loud, was admonished by Pavel. Dominic took a moment to compose himself again, then continued. "We were ordered to surrender with our army. Those who escaped to Britain did so in violation of their orders."

"As law is to justice, so orders are to duty, yes, Cichowski?" said Pavel.

York hesitated. On the other side of the wall, someone barked an order in Russian.

"We must go now," said Pavel. "Listen to me, Cichowski. You must do us a favor."

"What is it?"

"We are dead men. But you, Cichowski, you will survive this war. You must perform a service for Poland. Promise us that you will."

SNAPSHOTS

"If I can."

"Remember the Katyn Forest, Cichowski."

"Remember the Katyn Forest," Dominic added.

"Remember the Katyn Forest," repeated Pavel.

"The flower of Poland," said Dominic.

"Will you do that, Cichowski?"

"I will."

"Good," Pavel concluded. "I hope you get home."

"I hope you find peace."

York watched through the crack as feet, some bare, some wrapped in rags, shuffled past. He watched until the last man had gone.

Minutes later York entered the cottage. His four crewmates had taken their seats around the table, and Mikhail had just commenced ladling the contents of the pot into their bowls. York closed the door.

"Emmens," he quietly called.

Emmens looked up from his bowl as York tossed something to him, which Emmens snatched from the air. He opened his hand to find Ski York's West Point class ring.

The crude little cottage sat blacked out and nearly invisible in the night. The front door quietly opened, and Emmens stepped over the threshold. He carried a dim lantern under a blanket, which he removed after quietly closing the door behind him.

From the front porch, he waved the lantern from side to side.

From somewhere deep in the darkness, an engine started. Though faint and distant, the engine's deep and rough growl indicated a truck.

Emmens extinguished the lantern and set it aside. York, Herndon, Laban, and Pohl then silently filed out of the cottage, down the steps, and into the blackness—each man carrying a bundle of his possessions. The five made their way through the front gate and onto the road. The crunching of their shoes on the gravel was the only sound as they shuffled toward the engine noise.

In a minute or two, they reached the truck idling along the road. It was equipped with a canvas cover over the bed, and its lights were off.

A man jumped out of the bed and greeted Emmens. In the blackness York could only presume it was Abdul from the market. The man directed the Americans into the back of the truck, then closed the tailgate, unrolled the canvas flap, and buckled it to the gate.

"You sure we'll make the Persian border before sunup?" York whispered to Emmens as they settled onto the hard bench seats.

"We'd better," Emmens replied.

Abdul climbed behind the wheel and ground the truck into gear. It slowly moved away into the blackness.

Back in the cottage, Mikhail snored peacefully on the small couch, fully clothed, an empty vodka bottle on the floor nearby. On the table across the room, York had left a note addressed to William Standley, United States Ambassador, Moscow Mission, Union of Soviet Socialist Republics. It read:

SUBJECT: VIOLATION OF LAWFUL ORDERS

MR. AMBASSADOR: I FULLY ACKNOWLEDGE THE VIOLATION OF MY ORDERS. I AM PREPARED FOR THE CONSEQUENCES.

RESPECTFULLY SUBMITTED,

Edward C. York, Captain, United States Army Air Corps

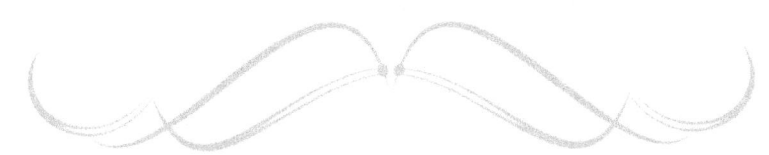

P AUL D. BURGESS'S CHILDHOOD WAS spent in a constant to-and-fro transit between the Rocky Mountain west, and the diversity of the Hawaiian islands, with a couple of years in Malaysia for good measure.

Inheriting the family wanderlust, Paul spent his early adult years traveling, first in the Marine Corps, then adventuring as a "freelance photojournalist" in Afghanistan in 1984.

Paul began that chapter in 1995 on the staffs of two US senators from the state of Wyoming, Alan Simpson and the late Mike Enzi. From there, he moved to the Pentagon to speech-write for Under Secretary of Defense Pete Aldridge.

Two years after the attacks of 9-11, Paul moved up to the White House to serve on staff with the National Security Council as speechwriter to Director Condoleezza Rice and her successor, Steve Hadley. At the same time, he performed regular assignments as Foreign Policy and National Security speechwriter to President George W. Bush.

Following his departure from the political arena, Paul spent the next fifteen years as speechwriter to CEOs within the nation's aerospace and defense companies.

Retiring from speech writing in 2021, Paul now focuses on novel writing.

*Former White House speechwriter Paul D. Burgess's debut novel, **Doolittle's Men**, was released in November of last year. The preceding short story is not excerpted from that novel.*

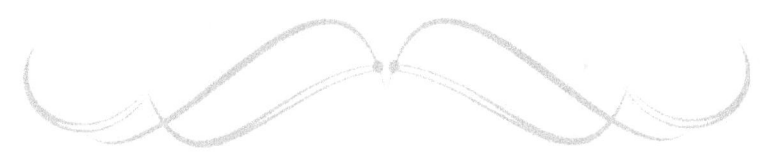

The Winch

Rudy Colomo Villarreal

AFTER COMPLETING MY US ARMY training in late 1964 at Fort Sill, Oklahoma, to become an artillery surveyor, I was sent to Germany aboard the USS *Patch*. Baumholder, where I was to be stationed in southwest Germany, was less than fifty miles from the borders of France and Luxembourg. Frankfurt am Main, the largest city in that area, lies about seventy miles to the northeast. By GI standards, Baumholder was the armpit of Germany. But I didn't know that at the time I boarded the southbound train for a ride lasting several hours.

It was beautiful and scenic, with snow covering everything. The countryside looked like a picture postcard. It was late in the day when I arrived at my destination. The last hour of travel had been by army vehicle. I was led to my bunk in the barracks that would be my home for the next seventeen months.

As I unpacked my gear, a sergeant whose name I can't recall, walked up and handed me a bottle of German beer.

"Welcome to Germany," he said with a smile.

It was a great welcome and calmed my nerves because by that time I was not a happy camper.

My unit, the 83rd Artillery, was attached to the 8th Infantry Division. In the infantry, a battalion is made up of companies. In the artillery, a battalion is made up of batteries. The 83ʳᵈ Battalion included a headquarters battery and several batteries of 105 *Howitzer* and 155 self-propelled cannons.

The survey section I was a member of was in headquarters battery. Each battery was billeted in its own barracks and the 83ʳᵈ's were all lined up together. The buildings were of German design, three or more stories, with several dormers projecting from the sloped roof. There were hundreds of barracks on the post. I suspect they had all been there since the third reich.

Baumholder was unique among the many U.S. Army posts in Germany because it was one of the few posts where live rounds could be fired. That resulted in a very busy post with the influx of not only U.S. Army units, but NATO units as well. It was not uncommon to see troops from Germany, England, and other countries conducting training exercises.

What made Baumholder so unpleasant was its size. There were 17,000 GIs stationed next to the town that had a population of maybe 2000. The majority of buildings in town were bars, and there would have been many more bars except each of our barracks contained its own bar.

Called "snack" bars, they opened for business in the late afternoon when our workday was completed and primarily served sandwiches, snacks, and German beer—lots of German beer. Those watering holes mainly were for the enjoyment of the troops, since the officers and noncommissioned officers (NCOs) had their own clubs on post.

Army life was routine and boring. Daily activity consisted of trekking up to the motor pool to maintain our equipment (unless we were scheduled for a training exercise or, heaven forbid, KP duty). Guard duty at night, which periodically came up, was also a pain-in-the-ass, especially during the winter months.

Three types of security clearances were issued by the government: confidential, secret, and top secret.

When I worked for the *Lockheed* Missile and Space Company, I had a secret clearance because of the nature of the job that required radiography (x-ray) of some classified hardware.

It's an expensive process the government goes through in granting a clearance. Government agents thoroughly investigate your background. I found this out when word got back to me that some "strangers" were "snooping" around Morenci, Arizona, asking questions about me. When I got to Germany, the Army completely went through the whole process again. There was a ton of money spent checking out little old me. Why the job required a secret clearance, I never completely understood. The only thing I could figure that would have been classified was that on guard duty, we sometimes had to guard the area where tactical nuclear shells were stored.

Since the end of World War II, Germany had been divided into West and East Germany. West Germany, where I was stationed, was a democracy and part of NATO and East Germany was a communist country and part of the USSR controlled Warsaw Pact military alliance.

Germany, like all countries of Western Europe, was heavily populated. Travel in any direction for no more than two miles and you would find a village or town. It was kind of overwhelming to anyone who was raised in the sparsely populated West and especially the Southwest United States.

While on a training exercise to Fulda, a town about ten miles from the East German border, our survey group was encamped in the forest west of there. We spent a couple of days surveying and obtaining coordinates of some of the prominent landmarks and features in the surrounding area. On the night before we were scheduled to depart for

SNAPSHOTS

Baumholder, three of us snuck out of camp and walked to a nearby village where there was a Gasthaus.

Every town or village, no matter how small, has at least one Gasthaus where you could get a meal or drinks. With me was Patrick Beaugard from Washington State and Bernau from Chicago. I can't recall his first name because no one ever called him by that—only by his surname.

We sat there quietly chatting and drinking beer when one of the other customers ordered a round for us. One good turn deserves another, and we reciprocated the friendly gesture. Soon we invited him over to join us and we began drinking his favorite combo—cognac with beer as a chaser.

After we had solved the world's problems and decided it was time to head back to camp, our friend insisted on giving us a ride. It was when we were outside that we discovered the ride would be in an *Esso* gasoline tanker. It was not one of the large gas tankers we have in the US, but a smaller version allowing the driver to negotiate the narrow streets found throughout Germany.

The tanker was half full of gasoline and we heard it sloshing around in the back as we drove through the village. I remember thinking that not only were we going to incinerate ourselves, but also the inhabitants of the small town. Our ride back to camp fortunately was short.

He deposited us near camp, bid us *auf wiedersehen*, and off he went. We were too wound up to hit the sack, so we climbed into Bernau's hutch—the camper-like enclosure taking up the entire truck bed of the vehicle he was assigned as driver. We sat there, softly talking and sipping beer from a flip-top.

The flip-top was a uniquely German bottle of beer that we GIs used to love. It contained a liter (about a quart) of beer. But what made it unique was the clever cap design. The ceramic/rubber stopper was held in place with a thick wire attached to the bottle's neck. To open it, you simply flipped the stopper off the end. The stopper remained on the neck and you don't have to be concerned about losing it. It easily snapped back on to close with an airtight fit, thereby preserving any remaining beer.

We must have sat there for about ten minutes when we heard a knock on the door. Thinking it might be our sergeant we quickly opened it. We were surprised to see our friendly *Esso* man.

batya—stock.adobe.com

He went on to explain he needed our help in extricating his truck from a ditch on the side of the road. Bernau quietly drove his truck over and using his front bumper winch, was able to set him free.

That was the good news.

The bad news was that in the process, the winch was damaged to the point where it wouldn't operate. Bernau was in a pickle. How was he going to explain the winch to our sergeant before the next periodic motor pool inspection?

The next day in the hustle and bustle to break camp and head back to Baumholder, no one, and especially the NCOs, noticed the cable hand loosely wound around the winch.

On the road, we traveled in a convoy of perhaps a dozen vehicles, with many pulling trailers. It was winter and the roads were slippery with snow and ice.

Bernau was driving his truck and next to him sat Patrick. I was with others in the back of the truck and of course the three of us who had partied the night before were dealing with a monumental hangover.

At some point the truck came to a sudden stop with a thunderous crash. We were all thrown forward, but fortunately no one sustained any injuries.

Our truck had plowed right into the rear of the vehicle in front. One other vehicle in the convoy had also rear ended another. It was an accident that might have been avoided had we been traveling slower under those conditions, but then we weren't leading the convoy and setting the speed.

It was an accident that had "damaged" the winch and conveniently let Bernau off the hook.

How I Ended up in the Artillery

Rudy Colomo Villarreal

W HILE DRIVING DAILY FROM MY apartment in Manhattan Beach, California, to my job at *Douglas* Aircraft in Santa Monica during the Cold War period of the early 1960s, I used to pass by an Army missile site located in Playa Del Rey. Observing the soldiers going through their early morning routine impressed upon me the idea that would be a great place to be stationed if I were ever drafted into the Army.

The *Douglas* facility I worked at was their missile and space division, where they built products for the military and NASA. I was employed as a technician in the Nondestructive Testing Laboratory, where ultrasonic inspection methods were being developed to inspect missile nozzles. With only two years of college, it was a great learning experience while assisting the four engineers also employed there.

One year later, I had taken a job as a Radiographic Inspector, x-raying missile components, at *Lockheed* Missile and Space Company (LMSC) in Sunnyvale, California. The *Lockheed* Missile Division was founded in early 1954, but it was the Soviet Union's launching of their satellite, *Sputnik* I, in 1957, that changed everything. That event, along with the Cold War, caused LMSC to boom.

SNAPSHOTS

When I started working there in January 1962, production was in full force on two major programs—the Navy *Polaris* ICBM and the *Agena* Satellite Booster.

The Santa Clara Valley, also known as The Valley of Heart's Delight, was paradise. It wasn't called Silicon Valley yet, although there was already a budding high-tech industry present. Companies like *LMSC*, *Hewlett Packard*, *Fairchild*, *Varian Associates*, and others would produce the seeds for incredible growth.

When I arrived, there were still remnants of the horticulture that had made that valley so pleasing. But the orchards of apricot, plum, cherry, and other fruit that had once covered the valley floor were rapidly giving way to urban sprawl.

The good life I was leading in the Valley of Heart's Delight came to a sudden end in August of 1964, when I was drafted into the US Army.

After giving my two weeks' notice at work, I sold or gave away the contents of my pad. I kept what I could pack into my *Corvair* for the trip to Morenci, Arizona where my parents lived.

Fort Ord was located on the south shore of Monterey Bay, less than five miles east of the city of Monterey, California. It's hard to imagine that a large military post could exist in such an idyllic setting.

Rolling hills of oak, pine, and cypress cooled by Pacific Ocean breezes. You couldn't ask for a better facility to be sent to for basic training.

That was the good news.

The bad news was Fort Ord was undergoing a quarantine because of an outbreak of spinal meningitis which confined us to our barracks during the hours we were not training in the field.

Under normal conditions, we would have been able to amuse ourselves by going to the post exchange, movies, or obtain a pass to go to town.

Basic training was eight weeks of instruction in the basic methods of soldiering. That included physical training, train fire with the M-14 rifle, first aid, etc.

Following basic training were eight more weeks of training in the special occupational duty we would perform in the infantry, or artillery, or armor, etc. For those and other military occupations we were sent to a special post equipped to train in those areas.

Toward the end of basic training, I learned I would be going to Fort Sill, Oklahoma—the Artillery Training Center—for my advanced phase of training.

At some point earlier, the Army had solicited my choice for advanced training and, naively believing I could be stationed at a missile site like Playa Del Rey, I chose missiles.

I guess the Army, trying to accommodate me to some degree, reasoned that if I was interested in missiles, the only area available for an inductee was artillery. I realize an artillery shell is a missile, but that was not the type of missile I had in mind. Perhaps had I been more specific and requested "guided" missiles, that might have made a difference.

Yeah, right.

SNAPSHOTS

So, that's how I ended up in the artillery.

I shouldn't be too hard on my Uncle Sam though, because in many cases they did place their inductees in jobs they performed as civilians.

* * *

My cousin, Raymond Grijalva, was an electrician in San Francisco and when drafted, did the same job in the Army while stationed in Greenland.

My brother Ruben was an A&P mechanic and when drafted, served in an aviation company in Vietnam.

I'm not too thrilled about the locations Raymond and Ruben served in, but then on that issue, the Army has rarely been accommodating.

At Fort Sill, I attended a school to train as an artillery surveyor. The function of the surveyor was to obtain the target information (coordinates) for the large cannons that fired artillery shells. In those days (1964) coordinates were still obtained the old-fashioned way—steel tape, theodolite, and hand computation.

The steel tape was used to get the precise distance between two points and required one surveyor on each end of the tape. The theodolite was a transit-like instrument with a telescope sight for establishing horizontal and vertical angles.

With that data and a known (given) coordinate, we could then compute, using tables of logarithms and anti-logarithms, the coordinates of the unknown point or target. It was a very complex, slow, and labor-intensive process, ripe with possibilities for error.

The electronic calculator, ubiquitous today, was not yet available, so we had to use special forms and add and subtract mentally to arrive at the results.

I'm not familiar with how the artillery obtains their target data today, but modern technology with computers, GPS, and more has surely made the way I learned it totally obsolete.

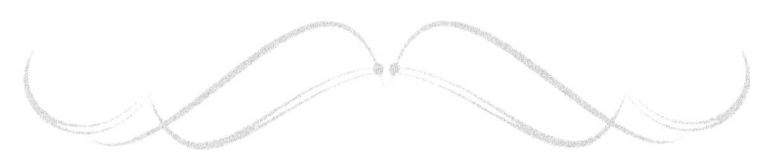

R UDY COLOMO VILLARREAL IS THE author of *Arizona's Hispanic Flyboys 1941-1945*, published in 2002 with a new edition in 2016.

More recently, he is the author of *Rare Bird: Hispanic Military Pilots of the USA*, published in 2020.

A graduate of Northrop Institute of Technology, he is retired after thirty years in the aerospace industry, having worked for *Douglas*, *Lockheed*, and *Garrett* Airesearch.

On August 27, 2022, *Rare Bird* was awarded a silver medal by the Military Writers Society of America at their annual awards banquet held in New Orleans, Louisiana.

CHRISTMAS STORY ~ 1969

Peter Adams Young

Christmas Eve brought the Bob Hope Show.
Four thousand of us squatted on the deck
Or perched on anything we could.
We screamed with laughter, shouted in applause
While warm, black water slipped by
Close outside.

There was a truce that night.
The decks were quiet,
Aircraft blind and dark.
Turkey in the Wardroom,
A few wild parties here and there
Celebrating life amid the empty bunks.

Others, too, we knew would celebrate,
Briefly safe in port.
They were sitting now

SNAPSHOTS

At drink-wet tables in the Cubi Club,

Staring at foggy windows

Black hills blacker still against the night,

Their ship lit up with "MERRY XMAS" lights.

Christmas Day was almost gone

When we came up on deck,

Moving stiffly in our nylon armor,

Helmets swinging.

The truce would end at six.

Our target time was 6:05.

Milestone Flight proceed to

Zero-eight-eight radial,

One hundred miles Channel 99.

Contact Nail Five-two on Button six.

The sun had just begun to gild

The pale karst cliffs.

Our target – troops, supplies, and trucks –

Lay safely covered in the trees;

A valley slope already deep in shadow.

Hodie! Hodie! Christus Natus Est!

Nail Five-two was good.

His voice, a lazy Texas drawl,

Talked us into easy contact.

His spot, a white, slow-curling smoke,

Hit right on.

He hung there

Far below us in his white-winged craft

And watched us work.

We gave him three runs – six bombs each.

Our second and our third were good enough.

The sun had still not set when we pulled off.

Nail gave our BDA as we both headed home:

Two trucks, two fires, four bunkers out, six killed by air,

And signed off:

A pleasure workin' with y'all,

An' a Merry Christmas to yuh, now.

Merry Christmas,

Nail Five-two.

SNAPSHOTS

The Eye of the Dog ~ 1969

Peter Adams Young

DAWN IS THE GUNNERS' TIME. The thick jungle night hangs in the trees with the morning mist long after the sun rises over the South China Sea. The forest remains deep in shadow while aircraft flying high overhead are bathed in the bright sun rays aloft. Easy targets.

The sun was still just a pink glow against the thunderheads on the horizon as we came up on the flight deck to preflight our plane. Still not enough light to see clearly, the deck was bathed in the red floodlights of night operations. My pilot and I, the weapons officer, stiffly moved in the warm, damp wind of morning, tightly cinched into torso harness and G-suits, and swinging our helmets by the chinstraps.

Our plane, an *A6-A Intruder* attack aircraft, loomed out of the red-edged shadows, huge and sleek and menacing in its stillness and bulk. Under the wings hung two dozen 500-pound bombs, their matte green shapes tipped with shiny brass fuses that winked in the thin beams of our flashlights. I checked each one: delay setting, arming wires, tail fins.

The flight deck around us crawled with movement. Planes were being positioned for the next launch or moved below for repairs on the deck-edge elevators. Plane captains and crews walked around their aircraft as we did, looking for the smallest discrepancy in the fading predawn darkness.

SNAPSHOTS

Grumman A-6 Intruder; Warfare History Network

A gentle but compelling lurch announced that the ship was turning into the wind for the next launch cycle.

We climbed up into the cockpit on each side as the flight deck ponderously leaned away from the turn. The relative quiet of the deck was abruptly broken by the voice of the Air Boss over the loudspeakers—soon drowned out by the rising whine and thunder of jet engines.

The sun rose above the rim of the horizon just as we were flung down the catapult track and off into the morning air. Once free of the deck the aircraft briefly settled and then started to slowly climb, clawing for altitude while carrying its load of over six tons of bombs.

We concentrated on following our departure pattern as we climbed higher and higher into the morning sun, secure in the constant chatter over the radio and the steady rumble of our engines. We crossed the narrow Northern neck of South Vietnam at the ancient city of Hue. Feet Dry.

The huge air base at Da Nang was a sprawling island of light on the coastline to our left. The dark, hostile masses of North Vietnam and Laos spread out to the North and West, dark but lit here and there by the fires set by exploding weapons or downed planes. Newer fires blazed intensely with white-hot centers, the occasional secondary explosion sending out tendrils of flame into the surrounding darkness. Older fires stretched in widening ragged circles under the heavy forest canopy.

No one was trying to put them out. They would burn until exhausted or stopped by a river.

We flew west into the remnants of the night, the rising sun painting our backs and reflecting off the polished plastic of our canopy. Below us, narrow, sluggish rivers snaked through the jungle—wandering trains that gleamed dully as if left by snails.

The thick morning mist rose from the damp jungle floor and hung in the treetops, wispy as Christmas angel hair. Another hour would pass before the sun could peek over the low coastal mountains and penetrate the shadows that clung to the bush. Even then, the gloom would only reluctantly give up, and hung in pools of shadow under the trees.

We saw nothing on the ground but the winding ribbons of water that wound through the low hills. Hidden within was the network of dirt roads and tracks that made up the Ho Chi Minh Trail.

Radio contact and twenty minutes of flying brought us to a rendezvous twenty-eight thousand feet above a featureless spot in the jungle, south of the abandoned town of Tchepone. Our airborne Forward Air Controller flew above us in wide circles, waiting for our arrival. He was Blind Bat 2-2, a converted C-130 transport equipped with infrared spotting gear. We were his last sortie before he could head back to base in Thailand. It had been a long night for Blind Bat, and he was impatient to be heading home.

"Okay... we've got some trucks," radioed Blind Bat. We were still miles and minutes away. *"Trucks and supplies in the open."*

SNAPSHOTS

It sounded too good to be true. There were seldom any clear targets on the trail, especially in daylight. Blind Bat described the target area as we approached—a meandering river bend outlined the rough shape of a dog's head below, bulbous snout and all. The trucks sat near the dog's muzzle at the end of a long tree line. Maybe they had been surprised by Blind Bat while unloading. No trucks drove the trail in daylight.

"Any guns in the area?" I asked as we caught sight of Blind Bat circling well to the west of the target area.

They radioed back they had seen none since arriving in the area, and nothing came up as we moved over the dog's head. We made a wide circle, getting in position for a dive.

The sun was fully up on the horizon, a coppery, blazing disk low in the eastern sky. The dog's head was still just a dim outline below. A few thin clouds streaked by us as we looked for the target in the gloomy mass below us.

"*Just put a few bombs about halfway down the nose next to the river*," Blind Bat suggested. "*I'll talk you in from there.*" He was eager to get us off target and headed home so he could head for the barn himself.

We took one more turn around the target area before rolling in. The plane briefly hung in the full sun, nose in the air, before falling into the steep glide of the dive-bombing run. I began the litany made second nature by long practice, calling off the altitude as my pilot concentrated on the aiming point.

"Master Arming Switch is 'on' passing twenty-two thousand... twenty-one... twenty..."

The fifty-degree dive angle felt almost vertical as we plunged toward the dark jungle below us. We hung against our shoulder straps, speed increasing in the dive as the ground came up, dark green and black.

"Nineteen... eighteen... seventeen..."

A stuttering white flame spit out of a grove of trees to our left, and a string of seven cherry-red glowing balls rose to meet us—slowly at first but rapidly gaining speed as they arced up into the morning sky. Soon tracers were streaking past us, past our wings, past the canopy. I could swear they hissed as they shot past, close enough to touch. Another burst followed a few seconds later, then a third—a steady sequence of tracers flashing by as we held into our dive path. A telltale column of light gray gun smoke drifted up out of the trees two miles below us.

"*Look out! They're shooting.*" Blind Bat came over the radio, his voice already shrill and strained with excitement. "*Two, maybe three guns—right in the eye of the dog.*"

"We see it," was all we could manage as a fourth burst of tracers hissed past us.

A small but certain lurch to the left and we were pointing at the cloud of gun smoke in the trees.

"I'm on the guns. Give me everything," my pilot said, concentrating on his aim point. "This is gonna be 'one pass—haul ass'."

I reached for the arming panel and pulled down the switches that would drop our full load of bombs. We were committed to the dive. I continued my chant, "Fifteen... fourteen..."

Only one in four anti-aircraft shells was a tracer they had told us. One in four. Still the strings of bright balls snaked straight at us, sliding by us between canopy and wingtips.

"*Hit 'em! Hit the guns.*" Blind Bat fairly screamed over the radio. "*Put it all in the eye of the dog.*"

"Passing ten... nine... Pickle and pull. Pickle and pull."

The plane gave a shudder as the bombs dropped away in rapid order. My pilot pulled hard on the stick as we knotted our guts against the sudden strain of the climb.

SNAPSHOTS

Six tons lighter, the plane soared up into the bright sky of morning, clawing for the safety of altitude as a final stream of tracers chased past us.

The bombs took half a minute to fall. Their impact was signaled by a sudden shock wave that ballooned and spread out from the center in a growing circle, pushing the ground fog and foliage out in front of it. Immediately afterward, a smoky ball of orange flame boiled out of the trees where the gunfire had originated. Even as the high explosive fireball began to collapse on itself, a white-hot fountain burst out of its center, sending fiery fingers outward in every direction.

Ammunition was hit and exploding on its own.

Weapons gone, we pointed the nose to the northeast, heading back to the ship as Blind Bat turned to the west.

"*Great shooting, gents,*" Blind Bat said in parting, "*Our guess is that was an out-and-out flak trap. The gomers are starting to get sneaky. We'll give you three thirty-seven/fifty-seven guns destroyed, multiple secondaries, and at least twelve KBA... A pleasure doing business with you.*"

My pilot looked over and slapped my thigh. How many men in a gun crew?

Behind us in the gathering light of the new day, the baleful yellow eye of the dog continued to blaze.

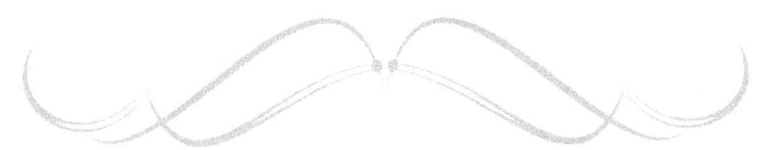

Jet Wreckage; Crewmen Found

Peter Adams Young

The story was buried on D-19,
Above a discount furniture ad,
Boxed in by a night school come-on.
An AP feed, barely three column inches.
I didn't know him all that well,
And, besides, it's been a while,

But his name called up a face.
He had a serious air about him,
And a Gildersleeve laugh when he'd had a few.
I think he liked to fish.

He'd found a piece of the Blue Ridge Mountains
Wednesday night,
And bought it. Planted himself
With his six-point-nine-million-dollar-airplane
And some guy I didn't know who was my age.

SNAPSHOTS

It took three days to reach the spot

He'd found so quickly

Less than half an hour after launch.

The story mentioned thunderstorms.

The why of it doesn't matter I suppose.

Suffice it to say

The sky failed to sustain them,

Or the ground rose up against them,

Or both.

I think someone once called the Blue Ridge

A poor excuse for a mountain range.

And when you think how he had played

Among the Cascade and Olympic peaks,

It does seem odd

That those worn-down hills could claim him.

But he was There, and knew how well

That poor excuse for a war

Could do the trick on anyone – plant

Just as deep in alien ground,

Or scatter, unremembered,

On the hot, wet wind that came across the Gulf.

How good you were had nothing to do with it.

Some of us survived – and he was one.

So, after these ten years of grace,
Twelve miles south of some Virginia town
And three days away from any living soul,
He ended it.
It ended him.
And I, ten years away and firmly on the ground,
Still wonder:

Why the hell did he stay with it?
How could I have left?

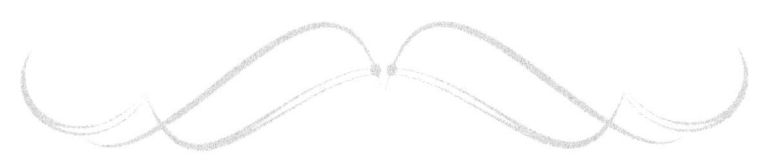

PETER ADAMS YOUNG IS A native of Washington, DC. After graduating from the US Naval Academy, he trained as a bombardier/navigator and flew nearly one hundred combat missions over Laos and North Vietnam.

Pete left the Navy in 1977 and began a career in the design and development of military command and control systems while sporadically working on his writing.

After living in San Diego, California, and Portland, Oregon, he and his wife retired to southwestern Washington state.

Pete is the author of *One Hundred Stingers*, a novel of the US air campaign against the Ho Chi Minh Trail during the Vietnam War, which was awarded a bronze medal in 2021 by the MWSA.

He is active in various veterans' groups and is currently working on the first of a series of contemporary murder mysteries set in and around Civil War battlefields.

FANNY COOPER: A WAR MOTHER'S STORY

Joan Ramirez

I F EVER THERE WAS A mother who should be given recognition as a person of merit, it is Fanny Cooper,
my World War II veteran uncle's mom. After fleeing
antisemitic persecution in the Austro-Hungarian Empire,
Fanny came to America in 1908 for a better life. With
only a winning smile and the ability to weave magic with
thread and needle, Fanny built a small seamstress business.

When Isaac Cooper walked into her shop on the Lower
East Side of Manhattan, he was smitten with her. Soon
after, they were married. As their marriage grew in years
so did the size of their family. At the time of Isaac's death,
Fanny cared for eight children.

Aside from the brownstone in Brooklyn Heights and a
small savings account, until her children were old enough
to contribute, Fanny was the breadwinner. Between her
work for small apparel shops and toiling away on her own
sewing machine, Fanny brought in enough money to put
food on the table and clothe each child.

The two oldest, William and Harry, became partners
in a pharmacy which filled the medical prescriptions of
the entire neighborhood. My Uncle William once told me
that Fanny's care packages of chicken soup and brisket
fortified him throughout his college years and later when
he served his country as a medic in World War II.

SNAPSHOTS

William and Cecilia were the jewels in the crown of the Cooper family. Fanny barely graduated from high school in her native Budapest because she was born at a time when women weren't encouraged to obtain higher education. Had she been able to acquire more training, she'd have been the first woman president in the United States, of this I'm convinced.

Tall in stature and vivacious in personality, her presence brightened every room of her home in her adopted Brooklyn. A champion of the underprivileged, she continued the family tradition of her native land to help those in need. Her ability to converse in Hungarian, German, Polish, and English motivated her children to learn other languages.

William walked the floors at night to complete his pharmacy education, at one point plagued by pleurisy. As the patriarchs of the Cooper family after grandfather passed away, William and his older brother, Harry, became the protectors of their siblings.

Harry, the more flamboyant brother, ruled with an iron hand. A confirmed bachelor, he saw it as his duty to be a strict disciplinarian. Unfortunately, that included his mother.

Other than brief outings to upstate New York Catskill resorts during the summer, Fanny never removed her apron. Seven days a week, with only breaks for the Sabbath, she could be found in the kitchen, cooking meals for Harry and William to take to the pharmacy.

When William, the younger brother, made Harry aware that "even God rested on the Sabbath," he became enraged.

Without a formal education and monetary reserves to fight back, Fanny was often confined to the kitchen to do Harry's bidding.

However, Willie more than compensated for whatever empathy Harry lacked. He left the immaculate neck bones of every turkey that Fanny cooked for him as a tribute to her culinary gifts. Not even the smallest plate of food went unacknowledged.

He also sent gifts from his time as a pharmacist in a medic post in Italy.

For the few leaves that Willie was granted, Fanny spent part of the time darning socks and sending him back to the troops with a fresh supply of necessary garments.

Fanny was no stranger to harsh words or struggles. Having fled her native land, she often wondered how one son could be so distant while the other was so loving.

Once she became an American citizen, she retold her story of losing William to the war effort. The nightmares of early survival that had plagued her but disappeared when she'd married Isaac Cooper returned after her beloved William was drafted in World War II.

Fanny went to the recruiting office and pleaded with the on-duty officer to spare her son from the ravages of war.

His response stunned her. "Every able-bodied man must serve his country in war as well as peace."

So began a hellish four years during which her only contact with William, who administered medical aide to his comrades, was postcards from his tours of duty in North Africa and the Italian campaign.

Fanny kept the Cooper household running as efficiently as Mussolini's train, stealing moments to read William's letters of comfort and open his gift packages.

When a telegram arrived, that Willie might have perished in a downed battleship, Fanny went into diabetic shock. Fearing her demise, Harry softened his stance. She survived, but diabetes continued to plague her for the remainder of her life.

With the news of William's survival, his older brother reverted to the status quo, barking out orders as though he were the commander of a battleship.

SNAPSHOTS

Fate stepped in to wipe away the tears that Fanny had shed for her beloved son. In September of 1945, her youngest daughter, Cecelia, treated her to a beauty parlor visit. As Cecelia fastened the pearls that Fanny wore only on special occasions, she wondered what the sudden fuss was over a Friday night family dinner.

"Until William comes home, it won't feel like a real gathering."

"Patience, Mother," Cecelia said, leading her down to the kitchen to help prepare the dinner table.

A familiar figure in uniform stood with his back to Fanny as she approached.

William turned to greet her.

"Hello, Mama."

From the moment Fanny set eyes on her favorite son until she passed away, each day she thanked the Lord for returning William, unharmed, to her.

I'd like to think it was a guiding hand on Fanny's shoulder who listened as she prayed for her son's safety and rewarded her for keeping the faith by delivering him back home.

J OAN RAMIREZ HOLDS A MASTER of Science in business, medical, and technical journalism as well as
two others in English as a second language and ele-
mentary education/autism.

She has published on a variety of topics from cochlear
implants to the economy and has conducted workshops
–domestic and foreign (Japan, Hong Kong, and South
Korea)–on the nuances of business communications for
managers and start-up companies.

She is the author of five fiction and non-fiction books/
novels in multi-genres as well as short mystery stories.

HUMAN TRAFFICKING

James Reddig, AKA *Vic Socotra*

The Navy Annex, Arlington, Virginia

04 September 2006

MILDRED "MILLIE" DOYLE WOULD HAVE had a sensible recommendation that would work on this military assignment piece. I never knew what her title was. General Services, Grade 13, I think. We had a joke about the assignments process in the Naval service. Back then, we jocularly called our trade "Flesh Peddling".

SNAPSHOTS

The term was a mildly ribald reference to a trade that was ended by force of arms in our Civil War. Better said, it was ended for a while, since news from what we can see happening on the border this morning, the flesh trade is back. It is called other things, mostly less offensive. The one they use in the media is "Human Trafficking", which could also be used to describe the DC Beltway. But the old phrase had a certain nautical flavor, which was useful when we were doing it.

Finding the correct officer for a tough job often meant a sales job in all directions, to the gaining and losing commands and, of course, the suspicious officers in question. That was not an unusual occurrence for the veteran community. As a matter of practice, on active duty, we normally packed up our desks every two or three years, sometimes with an ocean to cross to the next one.

That usually depended on how onerous what was coming next or currently was. From a family perspective, a pleasant alternative to the constant motion was to find a place with a lot of military jobs in the right career field and homestead in the area and live in the same house for a dozen months or more.

Of course, Norfolk was one of them, with plenty of ships and shore commands to bounce around in. DC had plenty of jobs with the opportunity for a homestead, but none were on ships. Still, an enterprising officer could craft a career that would only mean finding one or two sea tours and renting the house out while they were gone doing career progression.

Millie knew all about that since she had written the orders for whoever was Director of Naval Intelligence several times. And we all knew her, even if we didn't know the admiral.

I can't say Millie took care of me, meaning us, but raising or growing up in a military household was a challenge.

My sons were both born in Honolulu, where the word *kama'āina* means something special. "Child of the land" are the words in local parlance. They mean something significant about being from the Islands and non-tourist.

We were lucky enough to have two jobs in a row there. The waterfront view from the lanai of our government house looked out directly over the placid light green water along what had been Battleship Row. Back then, only Arizona was still there. But in the years since, the mighty USS *Missouri* was retired to serve as the battleship bookmark—impressive as hell. On her sweeping deck, the Japanese surrendered, and she nestled astern the graceful white arch that surmounted one of the first ones lost to their attack.

I had been overseas for more than three years then, sea duty out of Japan and a fourteen-month one-year tour in Korea. There was some human trafficking logic to that. Most initial assignments in the continental US (CONUS) were three years in duration.

The Japan tour was only two years due to the hardship. In order to line up with those who served three-year tours back home, the detailer lined me up for a one-year joint tour in Korea.

My opinion about that is best left to history, but the reality was that I was the only LTJG with two years of sea duty and a year under the US 8th Army walking around Seoul. So, despite my junior status, I thought of Hawaii as a reward of sorts, and I got married to have someone to sleep with who spoke better English than I did.

With the Hawaii time, it had been a colorful ten years. What appealed to me in my negotiations with the detailer was the possibility of coming to the very office in which he worked. And then, in a mass of confusion leaving the pleasant Isles, I entered into Millie Doyle's royal domain: The National Military Personnel Center.

SNAPSHOTS

No one called it NMPC. That was an imposition of words slung together by someone working on their end-of-tour award up on the Hill occupied by something we knew as The Bureau of Personnel, or BUPERS in Navy-speech.

That was the only title Millie would use, and she was always correct, having been there forty or fifty years. The Bureau was then located in a sandstone-colored depression-era building of immense proportions. It was adjacent to Arlington National Cemetery and on the hill that looked down on the Five-sided Adult Care Facility (FACF), also known as the Pentagon.

When I reported, the enormity of what I was supposed to do suddenly became apparent.

I won't go into the myriad of regular challenges in finding a place to live or the awful cost in miles to get from wherever that wound up being to the place I worked, and suddenly with schools being an issue.

We wound up in one of the places we could afford. Maryland or the District was out of the question for a variety of factors. Although the commute looked challenging, Fairfax was the choice. The schools were better, and there was every possibility I would be working in DC for most of whatever time I had left in the service.

The family might have a hometown.

When I reported, I discovered I was suddenly the placement officer for all the ships, squadrons, commands, services, bureaus, and offices entitled to Naval Intelligence manpower. The position was not viewed as part of the flesh-peddling side of the business.

I was supposed to ensure the external consumers were happy and learn the middle names of six or seven hundred people so I could move over to the assignments desk and start talking to the people whose lives I would help shape in a year or so.

At the Bureau, Millie Doyle was our civilian secretary. Better said, she had us uniformed figures as rotational office decorations. She had been with the Bureau since it was an office in the Bureau of Navigation, which was a long time indeed.

She had been with the little tribe of Naval Intelligence folks almost as long as it had been a formal community. And we were the oldest continuously chartered intelligence organization in United States history.

She was already gray and wraithlike when I first heard of her as an ensign since she physically processed the orders initiated by the detailers, the junior and senior officers who brokered the orders for juniors in the grades of ensign to lieutenant.

Our captain handled the smaller number of lieutenant commanders, commanders, and captains. Our few flag-rank officers were appropriately handled elsewhere.

Millie knew the stress the office imposed on ambitious careerists. She considered us to be extensions of her children who were grown and gone from home.

It was a small shop, perhaps five of us at any given time. A grizzled senior officer, two lieutenant commanders of possible talent, Millie, who actually ran the place, and a second class enlisted intelligence specialist to attempt to keep up with her paperwork.

The captain handled relations with the director of Naval Intelligence and his willful staff on community matters. The captain also personally dealt with the egos of the senior officers.

The lieutenant commander who sat across the aisle from him did the scut-work of complying with the community management apparatus in Op-01, the office that ran big Navy's accessions, training, schools, planning for promotion zones, statutory boards, and the other sometimes

SNAPSHOTS

Byzantine administrative process put in place over centuries in the Navy department.

It was an interesting assignment if you want to learn how things actually work. Our system was quite complex, so finding out what works and what doesn't was a crucial skill. Flesh-peddling also kept you on your toes. People seemed to care a great deal about their lives and careers.

Millie watched the whole thing from her desk by the door, where she sat across from the yeoman who tried to keep up with her. There was a routine level of pandemonium on the ground floor, and it was good we were there since it made suicide by jumping out the window just about impossible.

There were always officers just stopping by when in Washington to curry favor. There were also regular frantic and sometimes paranoid phone calls from officers around the world in the deployed units and embassies.

Early in the day, as early as 0500, there were calls from Europe and the Med. Before that, sometimes, the disoriented call from Arabia or a watch center in Korea.

Late in the day, it was the Pacific Fleet on the phone. Honestly, that global enterprise never slept.

Strict accountability was necessary.

Millie provided the context from the old days. During the days of Vietnam and the draft, the service was not as relentlessly careerist as it was with the arrival of the all-volunteer force.

Some of the officers assigned to the Bureau managed to beat the system and order themselves to graduate school as their obligated time expired. At least one enterprising young man had orders cut to report to his home, there to await a regular paycheck for doing nothing.

Millie knew everyone in the great sand-colored brick building on the hill. Others called it federal building number two, and those of us who labored there called it the Navy annex, where the Henderson Hall end of the ten-fingered five-story monstrosity held the contrarian Marine Corps headquarters.

The entrance overlooked a peaceful knoll in Arlington Cemetery, where the residents seemed to have all the time in the world.

Whatever you needed, Millie could provide. She was human, of course. She would get frustrated when a new software update on the Officer Assignment Information System (OAIS) would be posted to the mainframe in the data processing wing. It would take her as much as a week to figure out the bugs in the system, the ones that permitted her to get around the necessary approval safeguards.

It was an awesome power, and she did not take it lightly. She wouldn't initiate anything on her own. But if convinced of the justness of the cause, she could write the most extraordinary of clauses into the orders. "Detach within twenty-four hours" was one of my favorites. I imagined the consequences of that provision when the orders showed up on the ship's message board in some distant sea, half the allotted time already gone in the transmission of the paper being read.

Mostly we were above reproach. But I discovered that you could do literally anything if it appeared to be in the interest of the service. We made a captain disappear overnight when a minor peccadillo appeared on a periodic security investigation—nothing criminal, just potentially messy and embarrassing to the service.

"For the good of the Navy" was another useful phrase we learned early.

Normally, we allowed higher pay grades to determine what that might mean, but a certain iron core of justice burned in all of us. No one was going to get all the good deals. The underdogs and officers who had done the hard and thankless jobs were supposed to get a break, once in a while, a good job or a quota for a coveted school falling out of the sky and onto the morning message board.

Now, some delicate matters remain. Perhaps some things should just be allowed to be buried in the dead past, just as Millie is now. But they say federal building number two will be bulldozed to make space for the expanding legion of the dead of Arlington Cemetery across the street.

So, imagine a young and highly motivated officer, one of a long line of such officers who were confronted with an unpleasant task.

It might have been something to the effect of a requirement to reduce the number of personnel in a particular grade to keep the pyramid on glide-slope. It would have amounted to a requirement to throw some officers off active duty.

"Send them home," was the phrase.

Obviously, the super-performers were off the table. The service needed to keep the best and brightest.

Then there were the good, solid officers who showed up for work, did their best, endured the deployments, and saluted the flag. They constituted the bulk of the community. They were good solid citizens who were called the pack.

They were the middle of the bell curve, and of course, the remainder made up the pack-minus. In other circumstances, they could have been either of the above categories, but they had somehow drifted onto the grim breakers of Navy life.

Maybe they were just inept in person skills, or perhaps they were good people who had encountered one of the little Napoleons who sometimes got a chance at squadron or ship command. Perhaps they were just not cut out for that life.

Privately, I considered that you only had a career until you encountered the idiot who would write the piece of paper killing yours. It was not much consolation, but only one officer in all the military goes out on top, never having been deselected for anything.

That would be the chairman of the Joint Chiefs.

Everyone else had something to bitch about, some bastard who had stood in their way.

Imagine an officer having to examine the records of those officers who failed to select for lieutenant, the lowest grade for which there was an actual promotion board and for which the rate of opportunity was ninety-five percent.

It was a non-event for the overwhelming majority of officers. It served as a sort of training exercise for the later and harder boards where the selection rate might be much less than half, and disappointment was integral to transitioning to something else.

At least that first selection board was a non-event for those who made the grade. The junior officer detailer was the other one who had to deal with the consequences. That officer had to call up the handful of people who failed to select and chat about their Navy future, of which there was precisely none.

Most of them just wanted to get out. They were near the end of their obligation anyway and, had they the power, would have cheerfully written orders to go home and collect a paycheck for the rest of their time.

But there was always one who didn't think that way. Wounded ego and pride dictated that they fight for a chimera of justice. I appreciated the sentiment, even if I despaired of the extra work.

I did not have the heart to ever tell the full truth, though as a general practice, I found the truth, however unpleasant, to be immeasurably preferable to lying.

SNAPSHOTS

Truth is a constant, although malleable and much more easily remembered.

It was not fair, but that was how it was for everyone except the chairman. Imagine the bluster and fulmination over the phone. Imagine that the regulations precluded change-of-station orders that might fix the situation.

Imagine two piles of paper on a desk in front of an open window when smoking was still permitted in federal office buildings, a full ashtray, and a phone with an earpiece that never cooled from contact with the human ear.

Imagine Millie at her desk over the lunch hour when anyone sane would race out of the office to be away from the phones. Imagine the contents of the piles of paper.

Two or three good officers had to be sent home to make the numbers work. One problem child had to be kept in order to mount a feckless attempt at vindication that would never come.

Imagine that someone asked a hypothetical question in the still air, something along the lines of, "Could separation orders be issued, out of the blue, without review?"

Millie looked up with that expression she wore when one of her children asked something stupid.

"Of course," she said.

"Within twenty-four hours?"

I can imagine her look of scorn. Of course.

There would have been nothing on her face as she sat with the attorney a year later since the Sphinx would have been more communicative.

She might have said, "The computer system would not permit such a thing. It is hard enough to make it do what it is supposed to do. Anything else would be quite impossible. It must have been a system glitch."

There was a lot to think about as the Cold War concluded. Much has changed, of course. Millie finally retired and is now in the ground near her former home in Maryland. I remember talking to another BUPERS colleague about her loss. The idea of being newly reported without her knowledge to rely on would have been a daunting experience.

The Navy may have waited until after her retirement to move the Bureau. There was a World War Two base out in Tennessee that was confronted with closure in what we called a BRAC Round.

That meant base reallocation and closure in conventional English, and spreading the Navy footprint around in terms of congressional districts was considered a wise service strategy.

That meant the selection boards were held far away from Washington, and where else could you help mold the maritime future and still visit Graceland?

God bless the civilians of the general schedule who were the first bastion of our democracy. Millie could do anything if she were asked. Nicely.

Copyright 2022 Vic Socotra

SNAPSHOTS

JAMES REDDIG, CAREER NAVAL INTELLIGENCE officer with service afloat on the Pacific, Indian, and Atlantic Oceans and the Caribbean and Mediterranean seas. Shore assignments included Japan, Korea, Hawaii, San Diego, and Jacksonville, Florida.

Of all the interesting sites around the world the best were seen from Washington organizing congressional travel to places like Port au Prince, Taipei, Rangoon, and Pyongyang.

Service in three wars and multiple contingency operations. Trained as an all-source analyst, James Reddig applies those skills in travel to experience and learns from everything.

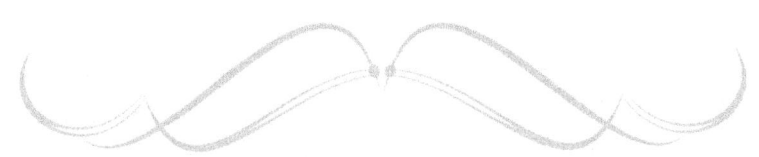

FROM ACTIVE TO RESERVES

Patrick Potter

A S WE CROSSED THE HUGE parking area toward the post exchange (PX), my buddy, 1st Lieutenant Frank Sharp elbowed me, "Look over there, at those reserve assholes."

I glanced past two rows of cars, toward the commissary. Two sorry-looking excuses for soldiers in soiled battle dress uniforms (BDUs), long hair tucked under their caps, shuffled toward the PX/Commissary complex. We couldn't see their boots, but they were doubtless scruffy.

"Yeah, I see them. We ought to go over and jack 'em up."

Frank replied in a slow drawl, "Shit. We could get their names, and report them to their unit, but it won't do a bit of good. Their commanding officer is probably a brother-in-law, and their first sergeant is, I'm guessing, a first f'n cousin."

I couldn't argue. reserve units, mostly National Guard but some U.S. Army Reserves (USAR), rotated into and out of Fort Knox from April to October for their annual training or AT. They'd draw M-60 tanks, M-113 Armored Personnel Carriers (APCs) and other armored unit equipment from post depots, then use it to conduct annual range qualifications, along with platoon and company-level field exercises. While on main post, and that seemed awfully frequent, an occasional reservist appeared

177

squared-away according to Army standards. Many, however, had a deserved reputation as a sorry lot, or at least
not spit-and-polish.

Seeing the reservists didn't trouble us for long. Frank
and I were in a perpetual good mood. It was the early
fall of 1979 and we'd both just returned from three-year
tours in U.S. Army Europe armor units—me in a border
armored cavalry regiment, he in a battalion of the Third
Armored Division.

Both units were high-priority, outstanding units,
although some morale and equipment problems still lingered from Vietnam. Basically, we'd worked our asses off
for three years, keeping our equipment and crews ready
in case the Cold War turned hot.

We worked easy hours in the Directorate of Training
Developments. That cushy assignment greatly differed
from being combat-arms junior officers in cold-war era
West Germany. I joshed Frank that as an armored cavalry
officer on the East-West German border, I'd worked twice
as hard as him. He didn't disagree. But he'd had plenty
of challenges, too, as a tank platoon leader and company
executive officer (XO).

He'd admitted that he felt lucky. He'd been newly
married when posted to Germany and was one of the few
who hadn't faced divorce amid the turmoil of Army life.
We were both glad for the Fort Knox downtime, living on
easy street, with long lunches and taking off early from
work on most days. Instead of manning and maintaining
tanks seven days a week, we commanded cushy armchairs
and desks.

We were both eligible for promotion to captain within
a few weeks. Before then, we had to decide whether to
continue our Army careers or resign our active-duty com-
missions. I was no waterwalker, so I knew that if I stayed
in, chances were, I'd find myself at Fort Hood, Texas for
another three fun-filled years with tanks.

Another alternative was to resign from active duty and join the Reserves, which desperately needed bodies according to the newspapers and what we heard.

But at that point, joining the Reserves seemed crazy. The reputation of the Reserves, both USAR and National Guard, was lower than whale-shit. Reserve units were full of misfits and good-old-boys, along with a smattering of Vietnam draft dodgers. Jokes circulated about nepotism in the Reserves, sometimes with three generations looking after each other in the same unit.

The Fort Knox newspaper, *The Turret*, frequently carried articles on reserve units. Many highlighted the citizen-soldier aspects, and the sacrifices made by reservists and their families. Some articles also covered how reservists often outscored active-duty units in tank gunnery. But that was a joke also—it was rumored that some reserve tank crews had served together for periods of five or more years. Active crews were lucky to be together for six months or a year.

The good times came to an end too soon. By mid-September, I found myself face-to-face with a no-nonsense chief warrant officer at the Fort Knox Personnel Activities Center. He held my DD 214 that would release me from active duty and grant me an honorable discharge from military obligations.

Abruptly he asked, "Are you interested in continuing your service in the Guard or USAR, Captain?" Clearly, he'd asked that question often, and he expected a fast response.

"Not really... But maybe I'll want to look into it later."

The chief slightly snorted. Not the yes or no answer he sought. "I'll put you down as yes and give you a number at Army Personnel Center in St. Louis, in case you want to find out about units in your home-town area. How's that sound?"

"Okay. Thanks, Chief."

SNAPSHOTS

Since I'd been an Army brat almost eighteen years, a West Point cadet for four, and on active duty for more than five years. I was happy to not cut all ties with Uncle Sam.

"Next!" shouted the chief. Lots of other guys like me needed out-processing.

Three months later, I'd made the move back to my home of record in Falls Church, Virginia. It wasn't my first choice, but I quickly settled into a pretty nice job as a contractor developing Army training systems. Happily, I found myself with mostly free evenings and weekends. But after a few weeks, I felt an obligation to call the ARPERCEN number to check on any good Reserve opportunities.

They provided information on units within an hour's drive of my home. One was a psychological operations outfit near Andrews AFB. I'd seen many articles on PSYOPs in various military journals. They worked with both conventional units and special operations units, and with foreign area experts.

Looking on the Internet, I found: PSYOP UNITS USE INTELLIGENCE SKILLS IN FOREIGN CULTURES AND LANGUAGES TO DEVELOP MESSAGES AND DISSEMINATE INFORMATION TO FOREIGN AUDIENCES IN SUPPORT OF U.S. POLICY AND NATIONAL OBJECTIVES.

It seemed intriguing. Maybe it wouldn't be a run-of-the-mill bunch of reserve yahoos.

I called the ARPERCEN guy back, and soon after received orders to the 7th Psychological Operations Battalion. I called their full-time point of contact (POC), Master Sergeant Grant, the battalion operations non-commissioned officer, to arrange a visit.

Taking along several copies of my orders, I found myself in front of a large brick building. The sign outside indicated the facility housed the 12th PSYOPs CO and 7th PSYOPs BN. The facility resembled a school, with a huge gym-like building at one end.

I soon learned the large structure was a drill hall common to almost all reserve centers. It could be used for drill and ceremonies, but mostly was used to park trucks in the shade or for pickup basketball games.

MSG Grant showed me around and introduced me to a couple of other full-timers, one in supply, another in admin. He told me to show up at 0730 in fatigue uniform for a unit drill the following weekend. He said there was a slot open for the battalion S-1 (administration), or possibly for HQ company commander.

My first morning of the drill weekend was confusing. My in-processing proceeded in a slap-dash manner, going from one section to another, sometimes processing, but mostly waiting around. I met most of the chain of command and learned in a round-about way that I'd be the battalion S-1/ personnel and admin officer for now but might be the HQ company commander soon. Based on whispered conversations, it appeared the current CO had dropped out of sight.

During my in-processing tour around the facility, I took note of the various sections and activities. Outside the main building, in the unit garage and storage facility, I encountered something familiar, the motor pool and its maintenance personnel.

It was a loud place, with the sounds of pneumatic wrenches and other tools, and a boombox reverberating in the depths of the building. Several mechanics, mostly young inner-city dudes, were enthusiastically working on a deuce-and-a-half, a *Jeep*, and a generator. They looked sloppy in greasy coveralls and T-shirts, but everyone concentrated on their jobs. It all seemed familiar from being in some armor units motor pools.

I then visited the supply section, again encountering mainly young Blacks from the local DC area. The atmosphere was quieter and included some females. Everyone seemed to be trying to look busy. Later, I found the mess section that consisted of more mature males, some looking overweight, intently working on preparing lunch at a series of polished stainless-steel tables and stoves. I saw that as I passed down the main hallway and looked through an open serving window.

Upstairs in the main building, I discovered the heart of the PSYOPs mission. Three large rooms contained safes, along with dozens of desks and tables strewn with papers, some with classified covers. Many walls were covered with maps, charts, and posters. Dozens of people worked and debated over the piles of papers and files or conducted training among themselves.

There were also desks and corners where soldiers struggled to look alert and involved but were catching up on their rest. Over time, I'd come to learn that many of the PSYOPs research and analysis officers and NCOs worked in government jobs in the heart of Washington, DC, at the Departments of State, Defense, Commerce, or the VA, AID, or USIA.

A huge room in the center of the building held two large machines that I learned were *Heidelberg* printing presses, capable of quickly producing hundreds of propaganda products: posters, leaflets, and other materials.

Two of the oldest and most unhealthy-looking NCOs I'd ever seen sat in comfortable chairs, smoking and nursing huge mugs of coffee.

It was rumored they were the only guys in America who could make the machines work.

A glance into an adjacent room revealed shelves of tape recorders and electronics, and a TV camera on a fancy tripod. A group of soldiers were engaged in animated discussion around a table. Snatches of their conversation revealed they were involved in a priority mission to prepare for an upcoming annual training event.

I made my way back downstairs with a sense that that was an interesting place, much different from standard Army units.

During the day, I participated in two company formations, and a battalion formation toward the end of the duty day. Being used to active duty, combat arms formations, I was surprised by the sloppy uniforms, inattentive attitudes, and a general sense of disorganization. It was also hard to hear given the side conversations and the movements back and forth.

At the back of the formation stood a file of soldiers in partial uniform or in PT gear. They were processing into or out of the unit or Army.

The last file of the formation comprised the unit's officers. Many of them were inattentive and several looked like they'd never heard of the Army weight control or physical fitness programs.

The formation became less military as word circulated that it would be the final formation for the current First Sergeant Kay Simpson.

She seemed squared away and in control. Most of the unit seemed attentive when she spoke, and all appeared sorry that she was leaving.

That was a new experience for me as armor and combat arms units had no females, and certainly none in positions of authority.

I didn't depart immediately after the formation, while most of the unit stampeded for the exits. 1SG Simpson sought me out.

"Sir, I see you're just coming off active duty. It probably doesn't seem to be that way, but our company is really pretty squared away."

I got the impression she might be trying to sell me on a commitment.

SNAPSHOTS

I couldn't agree with her at that point and said, "Well... it looks pretty raggedy."

She clearly expected that answer and patiently explained, "Yes, sir, but they work hard when you need them, and they look out for each other. This is a highly diverse organization. Nothing is very standardized. You have to go with the flow to make things work out."

My thoughts were still negative. "This unit is part of the U.S. Army, right?"

She continued, "Part of the problem is that I'm rotating out, and our HQ Company CO is... Well, he's missing. We hear he has legal issues with people in his apartment building, but no one seems to be able to contact him."

"Okay, but you have an alert roster and you, or somebody, will figure out what's going on, right?"

"Oh, yes sir, we're working on it every day. Maybe we'll know by tomorrow's drill. Oh, by the way, sir, at our last staff meeting we picked a replacement for me as the HQ Company first sergeant. Staff Sergeant Joe Barnfield, the guy over there."

She pointed to a SSG who looked like a disheveled rag bag in his Army fatigues and barely shined boots, with a mop of prematurely gray hair. But he seemed focused and was giving much-needed guidance to the soldiers nearby.

I wasn't impressed but all I said was, "You're going to have a staff sergeant as the company first sergeant?"

With emphasis, she replied, "Yes, sir, and he's a real good choice. He's a little older than most NCOs, has a college degree, and he's been to Vietnam twice. You give him a chance, sir, and he'll do a great job."

"Well, I'm willing to give it a try. I'll need to learn about USAR procedures from him, too."

"By the way, sir, coming off active duty, you're probably not familiar with the DA Form 1379, the RST form. I'll be glad to explain it because we use it a lot. RST stands for request for rescheduled training. So, whenever one of the soldiers has a conflict, they can replace either one, two, three or all four blocks of the training in the training schedule with other duties that benefit the unit and—"

"Wait, wait, wait, first sergeant. You mean this happens a lot?"

"Oh, yes, sir. Lots of the government guys have jobs that require travel, or have family vacations, or they have 'use or lose' leave time. And many of our junior folks have trouble getting transportation, or have lots of family events like funerals, or kids' activities, and so on and..."

I didn't hear the rest.

Damn! What have I gotten myself into? I thought.

I was going to have to make some serious attitude adjustments. The unit essentially relied on a bunch of civilians, many with work or family issues, including maternal ones. In combat arms units, females were non-existent.

A prevailing attitude in the active Army of the time was, "If the Army wanted you to have a wife and kids, they'd have issued them to you."

Luckily, I had a chance to briefly speak with acting 1SG Barnfield in the parking lot, and was quickly impressed with his knowledge, attitude, and clear maturity. In just a few sentences, he conveyed that he felt responsibility and concern for every member of the unit, and for getting the unit mission accomplished.

Driving home that evening from my first day of my first USAR drill weekend, my initial middling thoughts were of how to get the hell back out of this USAR disaster. I even briefly considered a return to active duty, where I knew the system.

But I calmed down and returned to a more rational line of thinking. I was deeply impressed by the words and actions of both the departing and the new first sergeants. In addition, I sensed lots of pride in getting the job done by many of the NCOs, soldiers and officers.

On reflection, I was starting to form a grudging appreciation for those citizen-soldiers, who fulfilled both regular civilian responsibilities along with key military duties. I felt a surprising sense of commitment, after such a brief exposure.

My next task—get the unit drill dates on my calendar at home, so I wouldn't have to RST too often.

SNAPSHOTS

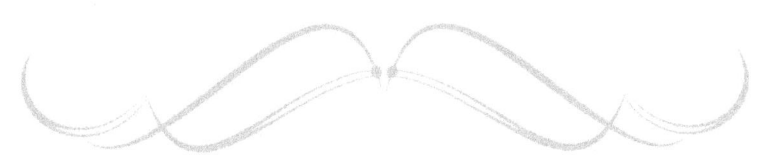

PATRICK POTTER IS A NOVICE writer but not a novice to the U.S. military. He spent eighteen years as an Army dependent, then entered the U.S. Military Academy at West Point graduating with the Class of 1974. He served over six years on active duty as an Armor officer mostly in an armored cavalry regiment on the East-West German border during the Cold War.

After active duty, he continued his service in the Army Reserves, mostly in psychological operations, civil affairs, and training units. As a civilian, he pursued a forty-year career as a defense contractor in northern Virginia, working a range of projects including operations research, equipment acquisition, risk assessment and threat analysis.

Mr. Potter and his wife live in Vienna, Virginia, where they raised four sons—one of which is active-duty Army and another in the Army National Guard. They also have a grandson and three granddaughters.

Escape Trigger

Bruce K. Berger, Ph.D.

*Opening chapter in my novel, which I hope to finish in 2023. The novel is titled: **Brothers Bound: Their Jungle Pilgrimage**.*

W E EXPERIENCED COUNTLESS CRUEL AND brutal acts in the prison camp, but we never imagined in our worst nightmares the cruelest act that would trigger our escape.

In the gathering darkness and a mosquito-choked pause in the monsoon downpour, Hues and I were returning to our bamboo cage from the crude outhouse nearby. It was our last trip of the day to deal with the diarrhea which haunted us often in our fourteen months of captivity in the small Viet Cong camp.

The site was invisible beneath numerous tall, overhanging trees in the jungled hills of South Vietnam, while the dense vegetation surrounding the camp limited sharply what we could see from the ground. So, we were hidden from the larger world above and blinded by the jungle maze surrounding us. We no longer existed in the big, so-called real world. We lived in a cage in hell.

We imagined the Laotian border was nearby. But there were no roads, road signs, or maps there. The sun, moon, and stars, when we could see them, were our only sense of direction in the rugged terrain. That and the memory of the helicopter crash site where we'd been captured near firebase Bastogne. That was located somewhere north-east of the camp—but no idea of the distance or exact direction. Miles of dense jungle and enemies between there and here.

It was a long two days and nights of forced marching through the jungle from the crash site to the prison camp. Or maybe more than two days. Time and distance had grown obscure. Our memories were increasingly frag-mented and blurred. Hunger, thirst, and pain were our con-stant companions now. Along with a growing desperation.

"Gettin' near the end of the line," we kidded each other. Nodding and smiling but deadly serious.

Time. Running. Out.

Our meager diet consisted of a mouthful or two of rice and some manioc root each day. On a good day, maybe a bite of fish and some fresh fruit. Period. The plague of illnesses we suffered ranged from diarrhea to Beriberi to fungal infections that painted red circles and square patches of itchy, flaking skin on our arms, legs, backs, and groins. Sometimes we felt we were scratching our bodies away, which delivered some brief relief. Followed by more pain.

I was carrying Hues to our cage that night. Three days earlier he'd severely damaged his left ankle when Caveman and Toothpick, our two guards, angrily pushed him down a slope on our way back from work. They did it to stop his Psalming—his musical renditions of biblical passages and prayers.

Hues stumbled, flipped, and awkwardly fell on his left foot and ankle. He screamed and then bounced twice more down the small hill, each bounce sharply banging his ankle. The guards then beat him into unconsciousness.

We weren't allowed to talk or scream in the camp. Our guards hated us. And vice versa.

We'd named the guards for their prominent physical features. Caveman was a short, burly man with thick muscles and a wide, flat forehead. His angry eyes were always lit with the fire of hatred. Toothpick possessed a pencil-thin body, strong but twig-like limbs, and empty, hollow eyes. One or both of them were our constant companions. Armed with guns. And bamboo clubs, which they often used to beat our permanently bruised bodies.

Later, after Hues' bad fall, the VC "doctor" rubbed some kind of gel onto his swollen and possibly cracked ankle. He tightly bound it in black cloth that matched the black pajama leggings and shirts we wore.

But Hues couldn't walk on it. So, I lifted and carried him. It was that, or they'd simply blow Hues away. We'd seen them kill several other POWs over the months who'd been weak, injured, and unable to work to gather food. Work or die. Nothing complicated. That was one of the most basic rules in camp for prisoners.

Our role was to gather food in the jungle and catch fish in the nearby river to help feed the VC and periodic North Vietnamese Army (NVA) teams who quietly used the Ho Chi Minh trail somewhere nearby to slip into the country and join the war. If you couldn't work, you were killed. That simple. And you could be killed for other reasons, too. Like talking too much. Disobeying orders. Stealing food. Acting defiant. Taking your turn in the Beat Down Ring. Or just for the happy hell of it.

Hues suddenly resumed his Psalming as we gimped toward our cage—an eight-by-eight-foot square, just four feet high, of bamboo poles tightly tied together and covered by a makeshift roof of poles, vines, and big leaves. He sang the religious words at the top of his deep voice.

He'd lost his mind again, or tipped over, as we called it. We both tipped over so frequently it was increasingly difficult to know when or whether we were tipped. We needed to escape soon, or we'd lose whatever we had left of our minds.

"Enough, Hues," I urgently whispered in his ear. "Don't make them any madder, man. We're barely hanging on now. Last thing we need is another damn beating. Or getting blown away like Rob and Ray. Stop, man. Just stop."

But Hues, whose leg and mind were wrapped in pulsating pain, though he wouldn't admit it, gave me a fierce but warm smile.

"The MAN telling me to shout out tonight, Buck," Hues whispered back. "I just living his words like he want me to. We got to get out, we ever hope to live again, Buck. My Psalms opening the door for us."

I started to tell him our escape was coming soon. But then I saw a burst of familiar bright light in Hues' brown eyes. The light of his spirit when it was on fire, which it was more and more. He broke into Psalming again, his MoCity Psalm #23. I'd heard them so many times I knew the words by heart:

"We living in the valley, shadow of death,

but fearing no man, nobody, nothing here.

The Lord he with us day and night,

filling our hungry hearts with love,

saying tonight it's fight or flight,

blessing our lives, shining his light, our way out."

Caveman and Toothpick angrily yelled at Hues to stop and get back in the cage. But in my arms, Hues continued Psalming, singing in a powerful voice.

Tipped over big time.

The two guards cursed and waved their thick bamboo clubs. Then they attacked and knocked me and Hues to the muddy ground.

Hues began low crawling away, finishing his Psalm in a deep mellow voice that ended in a whimper:

"Oh, Lord, I crawling into your Light tonight,

then my brother and my spirit, we walking home,

into love's embrace and forever life with you."

Caveman and Toothpick smashed their clubs on Hues' back and buttocks. Then they went for his head, which he tried to cover with his thin arms. They savagely attacked his shoulders and head, grunting and cursing as they swung. Again, they bamboo-whacked his back, arms, and head, like they were competing to see who could hit him hardest, most often.

They both won. Hues' lips stopped moving, and he lay still. Unconscious or dead.

Then it happened, the brutal, vivid moment that would live forever in my mind and drive our escape. The two guards knelt by Hues' head and waved a third guard over— Cross-eye, who guarded our cage at night.

Caveman roughly pulled and forced Hues' mouth open. Cross-eye then pinched and pulled his tongue out. Held it tightly.

Toothpick drew his knife and, with a quick twist of his wrist, sliced off a piece of Hues' tongue. He briefly held it out to admire his work. Then pushed it in close to my face. He bowed and grinned as he did.

Evil, evil eyes.

Then jammed it back into Hues' bloody mouth. Spit angrily on his face.

I lost it, then. Couldn't take any more of their torture.

I pushed myself up, lunged, and dove on the three guards. I threw weak punches with my left fist. Reached out with my right hand and tried to find and grab the knife.

SNAPSHOTS

I wanted the knife to kill them.

They'd repeatedly beaten and tortured Hues and me over the long months in the camp. I wanted to kill all three of them before they killed Hues.

Caveman grabbed his club and smashed my head. Pinned me to the ground and savagely beat me on my shoulders and neck.

I tried to block some of the punches with my arms. I was so damn weak. Too ill. Too damn battered to put up a great fight.

I cursed my weakness and cried out, "Stop it! Stop hitting my brother."

The last thing I saw as I turned my head before passing out—the red, red blood pooling in Hues' mouth just six feet away. Spilling over his lips with a rhythm of little hiccups. The small piece of tongue bubbling up and out. Sliding down his brown neck into the browner mud. It would play in slow motion forever in my mind.

The quick knife slash. Red blood spilling. The pink slice of tongue.

* * *

Later in the darkness and steady rainfall, I regained consciousness and woke with a start. I was panting and sweating heavily from a frightening nightmare: After they cut off Hues' tongue, Caveman abruptly shot Hues twice in the head.

The three VC guards then forced me at gunpoint to carry Hues to the Beat Down Ring. Cursing them and grieving for my brother, I dug a hole in the roiling mud. The three guards ripped off Hues' black pajamas and threw them in my face. Laughing at me and mocking my grief.

I gently laid Hues' body in the hole. Covered his body with mud and prayers. His grave.

196

They marched me back to the cage. Then cursed and beat me some more...

I twisted my head to the left as far as I could in my wooden restraints. They locked my head, arms, and ankles in place while I lay on my back. I glanced toward Hues' restraints nearby, desperate to see him alive.

In the near total darkness, I thought I saw Hues' black leggings, the edge of them hanging just above the ankle restraint. I looked toward Hues' head and faintly discerned a slightly darker shadow nearby that had to be his shoulder. Beyond that shadow was another darker shadow shaped just like his head.

Though I couldn't actually see Hues in the black night, I could feel his presence, just like I had for so many months in the cage. His spirit hovered close, and I could feel its strength. He was alive and still with me.

Apart from the rain, there was no sound. I imagined Hues was sleeping deeply in the soothing music of rain steadily rushing like a big waterfall. Probably snoring. He needed sleep. And a lot more to make it out alive. We both did.

I turned back and closed my eyes. Re-entered my troubled sleep zone, where I once again reviewed our escape plan. Hues wouldn't live long without surgery or stitches. No question. He needed help fast. A fact. And to do that, we had to escape as soon as possible, or he would die.

Another fact. We'd vowed to travel together, whether into safety and more life, or eternal death. Our commitment. I'd share the new timing of the escape with Hues first thing in the morning. Maybe help him feel better.

I had to make him feel better. He'd done so much for me.

We'd break out in the next few nights as soon as I could get back to the river to plant a decoy for our escape. We'd planned it for weeks.

SNAPSHOTS

We'd depart in the middle of the night. Hopefully, heavy rain just like tonight. I'd carry Hues every step of the way, if needed. We were brothers. We'd escape. Make it back home.

Together.

BRUCE K. BERGER, PH.D. SERVED in Vietnam in 1970 with the casualty branch of the 101ˢᵗ Airborne Division at Phu Bai. As next-of-kin editor, he wrote hundreds of sympathy letters to grieving families back home for the loss of their soldier that year. And sometimes he went with graves registration personnel to gather fallen brothers on battlefields.

His book Fragments: *The Long Coming Home* from Vietnam won an MWSA gold medal award for poetry book in 2021.

Today he's professor emeritus, University of Alabama, where he taught communications for seventeen years and was founding director of The Plank Center for Leadership in public relations. He's written/edited three books and dozens of research articles about leadership.

Before teaching, Berger spent twenty years as a communication specialist and executive traveling extensively and working on diverse projects in more than thirty countries for two international corporations—The *Upjohn Company* and *Whirlpool* Corporation.

Bruce resides today with his wife, Joan, and German Shepherd, Rose, near Tuscaloosa, Alabama.

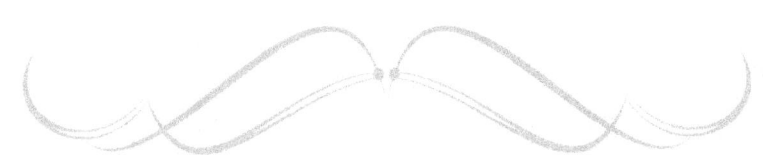

CLOSE AIR SUPPORT

Steve Stevenson

It's April 1968, just after the Tet Offensive in Vietnam.

"I'VE GOT THE FAC, TEN O'CLOCK, slightly low. Just above the dry creek bed," called F-4 backseater Captain George Watson, Gunfighter 2-1.

A flight of two F-4Es had been talking to Big 1-7 for the past two minutes, exchanging information, as the flight approached the target area in a valley east of the big A Shau Valley. The F-4 flight descended through 14,000 feet altitude looking for their Forward Area Controller (FAC).

"Got him," said Captain Mark 'Stodds' Stoddard. He radioed, "Gunfighter two-one has the FAC and is descending west of the river."

Captain Paul O. Dokken, Big 1-7, in a small O-1 *Cessna* Birddog, replied, "*Briefing remains the same. Caution for higher terrain west and just east of the target.*"

Paul Dokken was a FAC for the 1st Brigade, 101st Airborne Division, flying from Hue-Phu Bai Airfield, RVN. Dokken was known in the fighter community as "The Mad Dutchman".

Max "Bam Bam" Dawson was Gunfighter 2-2 in Stodds' flight. Dawson received his call sign due to his short, stout figure, red close-cut flattop, and resemblance to the cartoon character of the same name. He had been Stodds' wingman for over three months, and they worked well together.

Huge Randy "Moose" Mattings, Texas A&M Class of '64, was Bam Bam's back-seater. They made an interesting pair.

The flight of two F-4Es was Close Air Support (CAS) Alert, scrambled from Da Nang Airbase. 2-1 carried four Mk-82 500-pound Snake Eye retarded bombs, while 2-2 carried four 500-pound canisters of napalm. Both F-4s had a 20mm cannon.

Their CAS target that day was southwest of Hue, adjacent to the A Shau Valley. The requester was an infantry company of the 1st Brigade, 101st Airborne Division in heavy contact with a regular North Vietnamese Army (NVA) unit. The Infantry Company Commander's call sign was Demon 6.

Stodds: "Bam Bam, hold high at eight, and I'll stay below seven," as the F-4s descended around large cumulus clouds toward a narrow valley. That would give the F-4s a thousand-foot safety separation.

"Two copies at eight, going level, and I am receiving music from the west." That meant NVA anti-aircraft gun radar from the A Shau Valley. Unwelcome news if aircraft went into the valley at low altitude and/or slow.

Dokken: *"One-seven, yeah, the Huey crews report the buzz if they unmask anywhere east of the valley."*

Stodds: "Okay. Let me sneak around these clouds, and I'll be down there."

Cumulus clouds formed over the mountain peaks and ridges, threatening to turn into thunderstorms.

Afternoon thunderstorms were a standard weather event that time of the year, forming tall white tops to the green forest-covered valley walls.

Stodds circled a large opening between clouds until he had a clear view of the valley floor, then he stood the F-4 on its left wing and sliced down into the valley.

Up to 6000 feet in elevation, ragged, sharp, razor-back ridges defined the west side of this valley. The mountains were lower to the east, rising to almost 4,000 feet.

Stodds leveled and kept the Phantom in a tight racetrack pattern to stay in the valley and keep Big 1-7 in sight.

"This is not fun," mumbled George from the back seat as he watched the forest-covered ridges flash past the F-4's wing. Awful close for his liking.

"Just another day in the office," replied Stodds.

Big 1-7: *"South end of the valley, bad guys are bunkered in the tree line, east of the open field. The good guys are mostly on the west end of the open area except for a group pinned down in the center of the paddy behind a dike. Suggest south-to-north run-in. Ground commander approves 'Danger Close' drop. Big one-seven is ready to mark."*

Stodds: "Stand by one." On the intercom, "Gun sight mils set for Snake, stations selected, Master arm to arm. Green lights. Pickle at two point nine."

George responds, "Copy two point nine. Checklist complete. FAC is at eleven o'clock, slightly low, just below the west ridge line."

Stodds radioed, "Big one-seven, Gunfighter two-one is ready for mark."

Dokken: *"One-seven will mark in five seconds."*

Stodds watched the tiny *Cessna* O-1 roll left almost inverted, pull back to point at the northeast edge of the valley, roll wings level in a twenty-degree dive, and *BANG!* fired a white phosphorus rocket into the vegetation twenty yards from the forest edge.

SNAPSHOTS

A bright white cloud billowed up in contrast to the dark green trees. Yellow tracers reached for Big 1-7 but fell behind him.

Stodds called, "Gunfighter two-one has the mark. Inbound with Snake-eye in ten seconds," as he maneuvers under a growing rain cloud.

"Gunfighter two-two has the mark," echoed Bam Bam from high overhead.

Dokken: "*Ground commander confirms Snake. Keep it to the north of my mark. Cleared hot*"

"Copy north of mark and cleared. Two-one is in hot," as Stodds pulled the big Phantom around in a 4G turn to align with the target.

"Dive angle is good, airspeed is good," confirmed George.

As the gun sight pipper crawled up to the tree line and the white smoke, Stodds thumbed the release button on the control stick's grip for two Mark 82 high drag bombs.

George called, "Pickle."

The two Mark 82 bombs ejected from their racks, and lanyards attached to the bomb racks pulled the retaining bands around the bombs loose. Four folded fins popped open to retard each bomb's flight.

Stodds pulled his fighter up in a 4G climb until he had a positive up climb established and rolled left to avoid the ridge line and the thunderstorm brewing overhead.

* * *

For the infantry grunts hiding behind the dikes, the blast was massive. A shock wave rolled across the dry rice paddy, lifted the grunts an inch off the ground, and slammed them back down in the dust.

* * *

High overhead, Bam Bam saw an expanding white bubble of condensation grow from the explosion point. Compressed by the bomb explosion, the humid tropical air created the bubble, growing to 150 yards in diameter, where it finally dissipated.

George looked back to see the two explosions and the condensation bubble, commenting, "Good drop."

Stodds was busy dodging ridge lines and a growing thunderstorm.

Big 1-7 called, *"Demon Six says that was on target. Move ten meters south."*

"Two-one copies ten meters south." Stodds curled his F-4 back around for a second pass, flying level with the top of the A Shau Valley ridge line. "Two-one is in, in ten seconds," Stodds called to the FAC.

Big 1-7 relayed *"Fighter five seconds from drop"* to Demon 6.

That pass, 2-1's bombs hit about fifteen meters south of the smoke from his first bombs' craters. Blast results were the same.

Big 1-7, *"Good drop, but Demon is still receiving fire from the north tree line."*

Just as Stodds was about to call 2-2 down, Bam Bam radios, "Gunfighter Lead. Two-two lost sight of the FAC and valley. That thunderstorm is growing by the minute."

"Okay, stay at eight in the clear, and I'm gonna pop up to seven once I find a good opening." Stodds turned to the north end of his valley, made sure he had a good mental picture of the terrain and did a zoom climb in the clear just north of the massive thunderstorm.

Black clouds and a gray anvil head cloud lean over the valley.

SNAPSHOTS

As lead's F-4 curled up through a clearing in the clouds, Bam Bam called, "Two-two's got lead at my eleven o'clock low. Permission to rejoin."

"Cleared rejoin, wedge. Two-one is reversing turn, and we'll start down when you're in." Ten seconds later, 2-2 called, "Two's in."

Gunfighter 2-1 took the formation down, around the thunderstorm, and into the narrow confines of the valley.

George in the back seat radioed, "Two-one has the FAC in sight." Then on intercom, he said, "Geez, he's so low Charlie could whack him with a branch."

"*I will re-mark.*" Big 1-7 turned the little *Cessna* O-1 across the valley, and in a shallow dive from high overhead the grunts pinned down in the rice paddy, he fired another white phosphorus rocket into the trees. Green and red tracers chased the small aircraft as Big 1-7 turned away.

A pause, and then Big 1-7 radioed, "*Demon six says good mark. Nape on the tree line in front of the mark and going north. Demon six acknowledges Danger Close.*"

Bam Bam radioed, "Two-two has good tally on the mark. Danger Close. Fighter in, in ten seconds."

"*Cleared hot.*"

"Copy, Two-two is in hot." You heard the strain in his voice as Bam Bam pulled 4Gs to stay in the valley and line up for his drop.

Stodds radioed, "Two-one is climbing to eight thousand. It's crowded down here."

On target, Bam Bam's F-4 kicked two large 500-pound silver canisters from their racks.

The shiny napalm tanks slowly tumbled, end-over-end, toward the tree line. On impact, they burst, releasing a wall of thickened petroleum. A white phosphorus fuse in the container instantaneously ignited the cloud of fuel, creating a wall of fire over one hundred yards from the impact point and sucked up the air in the surrounding area.

The sound was not an explosion but an exceptionally loud, "*Whump.*"

The grunts behind the rice paddy dikes felt the temperature flash and air suction as the napalm ignited 200 yards away.

The Company Commander, Demon 6, cleared 2-2 in for another nape pass, just south of the first mark.

That was real Danger Close.

Big 1-7, "*Move it to the south five meters.*"

"Two-two, Copies south five meters. Two-two is in hot."

Bam Bam noticed the giant thunderstorm cloud had moved over the south end of the valley, bringing a dark shadow and light rain to the target area.

In the light rain and growing darkness, 2-2 dropped his nape a bit closer to the open rice paddy, with chunks of the napalm ricocheting off the palm trees. A tiny spot of napalm splashed one of the Demon's paratroopers (2nd-degree arm burn, treated, not evacuated).

Gunfighter 2-2 called, "Off-target" and pointed his Phantom upward in full military power to find his leader in the clear skies east of the A Shau Valley.

* * *

The Snake and Nape had silenced the bad guys. The 101st Infantry company rapidly jumped up online and assaulted the bunker complex. They received only four shots in resistance.

A strong petroleum smell, along with the smell of burned grass, floated in the air. They advanced through the bunkers, and the troopers found three charred weapons and one NVA soldier Killed By Air (KBA).

SNAPSHOTS

The second platoon searched the southern bunkers and found a sandal with a human foot still inserted but no body attached.

The Demon's company had suffered only one slightly burned paratrooper who wanted a Purple Heart Medal from the Air Force.

DAY TWO

That morning, Stodds flew as Number Two (3-2) to a target again just outside the A Shau Valley. The flight of two F-4Es (Gunfighter 3-1) was led by Major John McNeil, the squadron assistant operations officer. Although he had over 1,000 hours in the F-4, he had been at Da Nang for only three weeks and already had a reputation for not wanting to take chances.

The target area southwest of Hue was getting hot. There was a lot of AAA in the area, particularly from the ridge lines overlooking the valley. The NVA brought 12.7mm machine guns and a lone ZSU-23-2 anti-aircraft weapon to the fight. It was just over the edge of the A Shau Valley.

Captain Paul Dokken was again the on-scene FAC, call sign Big 1-7. Dokken was trying to help a 101st Infantry company attacked by almost a battalion of NVA.

After two passes each by the F-4s, with lots of ground fire, flight lead said, "It's too hot to go back into the target area. Gunfighter flight, rejoin."

"Three-two has ordnance and wants to make more passes." Stodds had heard Big 1-7 talking to the ground troops, who were in a world of hurt, with one platoon cut off and facing a large number of NVA troops. Stodds felt they had to go back and help the platoon.

Lead told him bluntly, "Two, rejoin. Now! We are going back to Da Nang."

Stodds pulled off his racetrack pattern without dropping, saw his leader well on the eastern side of the valley, and started to rejoin. He flew with a clenched jaw on the short fifty-mile flight back to Da Nang.

* * *

The flight landed on Da Nang's runway 18L, taxied into their protective revetments on the west side, and shut down. Stodds and his WSO climbed out of their F-4 without saying a word.

George had never seen Stodds that hot.

Stodds gathered his helmet bag, maps, and frequency cards and started off but turned back.

Stodds spit out, "You take maintenance debriefs. I am going to the club." His longtime back-seater knew better than to argue with Stodds.

Stodds was two scotches into fuming when Major McNeil walked into the Da Nang officers open mess

SNAPSHOTS

O'Club bar, known as the DOOM Club, trailed by Captain Watson.

McNeil opened his approach with, "Captain Stoddard, You should have gone to maintenance and mission debrief."

Stodds wheeled on him and said, "And we should have gone back and made more passes. We had ordnance but abandoned twenty GIs out there."

Major McNeil replied, "It was getting too hot to go back down there."

Stodds leaned toward his flight lead, so mad there was spittle flying off the corners of his mouth.

"We abandoned them out there. They may be dead now."

The major stood his ground and said, "Stodds, your job was to bring that five-million-dollar airplane back to Da Nang."

Stodds barked, "Bull crap! Twenty GIs were out there who needed our help, and you wouldn't do it. You wouldn't do it. Twenty GI's are worth a lot more than one stinking airplane."

George Watson stepped between the two combatants, facing Stodds, and stuck his fist in Stodds' chest. "Stodds, don't go there." He pushed his front seater backward, "Don't go there."

The normally raucous O'Club bar was suddenly silent. None of the other fighter jocks moved, but they turned enough to watch the confrontation at the bar.

SNAPSHOTS

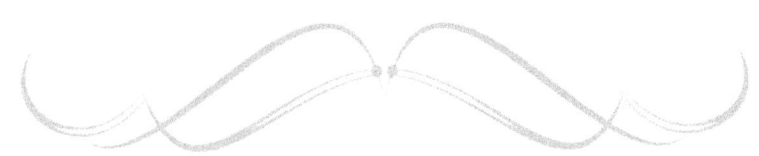

S TEVE STEVENSON HOLDS A BA degree from the University of Texas and a Masters of Public Administration degree from Auburn University. He is the author of *From Both Sides Now* and has written short stories for the military's *TAC Attack* and *The Daedalian Flyer* magazines.

A career military officer, Steve was commissioned through Army ROTC at UT. He served two tours in Vietnam with the 101st Airborne Division, commanding platoon and company-sized units in combat, and one tour with 5th Special Forces.

Steve then transferred to the Air Force for pilot training. He flew F-4s, A-10s, O-2s, OV-10s, OT-37s, CT-39s, and CH-3 helicopters and commanded at flight, squadron, and wing levels. He was a joint planner for several projects including the development and deployment of the JSTARS system.

Steve lives in Bulverde, Texas and is married to Claire, his bride of over fifty-two years. They have two grown sons.

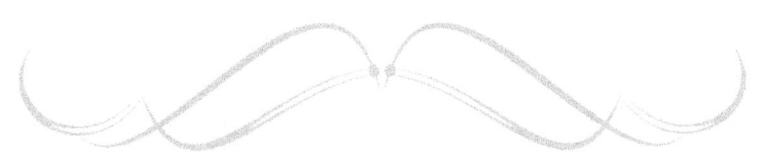

AT THE WRONG END
OF RIFLE BARRELS

John B. Haseman, Colonel US Army-Retired

IT WAS AUGUST 1988, AND I was more than a year into my three-year assignment as U.S. Defense and Army Attaché at the American Embassy in Rangoon, Burma. I had become a U.S. Army Foreign Area Officer (FAO) shortly after the end of the Vietnam War, when that career program was established.

FAOs filled assignments as military attachés, security cooperation officers, policy advisors, intelligence analysts, and in both regular and special operations billets from the tactical field to top-level command and staff postings. My assignment to Rangoon was my seventh consecutive FAO posting.

Rangoon was fifty years behind nearby Bangkok, Thailand, in terms of economic development, infrastructure, standard of living, and creature comforts. It was very enjoyable with its distinctive culture, wonderful people, and beautiful unspoiled countryside.

However, sadly, Burma had one of the world's most egregious human rights situations—an all-powerful and brutal army governed the country (very poorly).

All members of the small international diplomatic community had stories to tell of violence or other disturbing incidents between the government and its citizens.

SNAPSHOTS

But nothing prepared me for the events of August and September 1988.

I was chief of a five-person defense attaché office (DAO). Besides me, we had the air attaché (lieutenant colonel), operations coordinator (army warrant officer), operations NCO (army sergeant first class), and administrative NCO (air force staff sergeant).

Our embassy staff also included six U.S. Marine Corps personnel in the embassy security guard detachment.

My leadership responsibility encompassed not only our small military community, but also the entire community of embassy staff and their families.

We were particularly fortunate that Ambassador Burton Levin was a superb career diplomat whose leadership skills and people skills were repeatedly demonstrated during many months of tension and violence.

Tensions in Rangoon began to rise back in September 1987, when the government suddenly devalued the three largest-denomination currency bills—without recompense. Millions of people lost all their savings.

Army and police squads brutally quelled student-led protests. Police raped university students and beat anybody they pleased. Very small anti-government demonstrations sporadically broke out and were quickly dispersed. Tensions remained high throughout the city for months thereafter.

Then in July 1988, dictator General Ne Win suddenly announced he was resigning from all his positions, and the ruling military junta appointed the general known as the Butcher of Rangoon as the new junta leader.

Large anti-government demonstrations began almost daily, including in the plaza in front of city hall— directly across Independence Square from the American Embassy.

The demonstrations were at first tolerated, very unusual for Burma, where anti-government protests of any size were quickly broken up with violence by police or army units.

Then came 8 August 1988.

Sometime during the night of 7-8 August 1988, the ruling junta ordered the army to use force and violence to quell all anti-government demonstrations.

Those orders were not announced to the public, and there was no warning that violence was going to occur throughout the city of Rangoon.

The morning of August 8th began as an ordinary day for me. I left my official residence and headed to the embassy at about 7:15. Before my official driver and I had traveled even two blocks, a frantic call came over the car radio:

"Help! Anybody hearing. Help! I'm on Boundary Road in the middle of a huge crowd of Burmese, and the Army is shooting at me. Anybody hearing this, please help."

It was Len, the embassy administrative counselor, calling for help. We were only minutes away from the trouble spot, so I told my driver to step on it.

On the radio I told Len to lie on the floor of his car where the engine block would give him some protection from bullets.

We neared the danger area driving north on U Wisara Boulevard, a divided four-lane parkway with a grass-and-trees median strip.

As we approached the four-way intersection with Boundary Road, I opened the rear passenger-side window and heard the pop-pop-pop of rifle fire and immediately saw at least a dozen soldiers in the intersection and on the triangular-shaped island between U Wisara's main travel lanes and a right-turn lane onto Boundary Road.

SNAPSHOTS

The soldiers were shooting into a large crowd of hundreds of unarmed civilians fleeing east on Boundary Road, where my embassy colleague was stopped amidst the panicked crowd.

At my direction, my driver pulled partly into the right-turn lane and stopped but left the engine running. Soldiers blocked us and there were many more on the island.

I took my diplomatic ID card out of my wallet, left the car—leaving the rear passenger-side door open—and slowly approached the soldiers. Needless to say, I was immediately noticed—the big white sedan with diplomatic license plates and a tall Western man were hard to miss.

The rate of fire from the soldiers shooting down the street at fleeing Burmese—and the admin counselor's car—slowed but did not stop. Many of the soldiers turned to stare at the unexpected interruption and many shifted their rifles to cover me.

The officer in charge was a lieutenant or captain, I don't recall. I was not in uniform, rather I was dressed in my normal embassy work clothes—a short-sleeved safari suit.

I held out my diplomatic ID card, identified myself by rank and name, and in my not-too-good Burmese but in my very best military command voice I demanded the soldiers stop shooting "at an American diplomat in an official American diplomatic automobile."

I repeated the demand, firmly, in English, with gestures pointing down Boundary Road toward where the admin counselor's vehicle was stopped.

The officer told me (in Burmese) that I was interfering in a military operation, and to immediately leave.

I again demanded the soldiers stop shooting at an American Embassy vehicle.

By that time angry, the officer shouted in English, "You! Go! Now!"

By then the shooting had stopped, but too late for the dozens of Burmese lying in the street, dead or wounded from rifle fire.

Then, I heard another soldier tell the officer, in Burmese, "We could shoot him and claim it was an accident."

My driver also heard that, and called out loudly to me, "Sir, we need to get out of here right now."

I was ready to leave. I walked slowly to the passenger side of the car but never turned my back on the soldiers. Several of them put their hands on me and shoved me into the rear passenger seat of the sedan.

I pulled the door closed.

One soldier stuck his rifle barrel through the open window. I told the driver to back up and get us the hell out of there.

My driver backed up, quickly turned, and headed south toward the embassy in the northbound lanes (driving the wrong way) on U Wisara Boulevard.

I used the car radio to alert "all monitoring this frequency" of violence on the streets and to return to their quarters and not to attempt to drive to the embassy.

At that point, I did not know what was happening elsewhere in the city. The confrontation between me and well over a dozen armed Burmese army soldiers was the first indication any U.S. diplomats had about violence in the streets of Rangoon that morning.

At the embassy, I quickly went upstairs to the ambassador's office suite and telephoned Ambassador Levin to describe what had happened.

He in turn opened our telephonic warden notification ladder system and told all Americans to remain at home until further notice.

SNAPSHOTS

Then, I telephoned the chief of the Burmese Armed Forces (known as Tatmadaw) Foreign Liaison Office (FLO) and delivered a formal protest about the shooting on Boundary Road that endangered the life of an American diplomat, and my treatment at the hands of the soldiers there.

["Tatmadaw" is a Burmese term that refers to the institution of all defense forces.]

I told him what I had observed and done and re-emphasized the official protest of shots fired at a U.S. diplomat, even though he was an innocent victim trapped amid the fatal shooting of dozens of unarmed civilians, and armed Burmese soldiers putting their hands on a senior American diplomat and threatening me.

The FLO chief immediately issued a formal verbal protest at my actions "interfering with the proper duties of the Tatmadaw."

Word had traveled fast from that officer at Boundary Road—at least he had correctly reported who I was. The Burmese government official note criticizing my behavior arrived at the embassy later that afternoon.

We soon learned from a continuous stream of in-coming telephone calls from Burmese citizens that there had been a large anti-government demonstration at the Shwedagon Pagoda—the most important religious edifice in Burma. The army unit I had encountered was but one of many that, overnight, had been ordered to use deadly force to break up protest demonstrations.

At almost the same time as the Boundary Road incident, a crowd of civilians on the plaza in front of city hall was fired on by soldiers ordered to disperse them.

The government declared martial law, forbade any gathering of more than five people, and began an overnight curfew, initially from 4:00 P.M. until 6:00 A.M. the next morning.

Another embassy staff officer and I went up onto the roof of the embassy, where a sturdy wooden platform built between two window gables gave us a view across Independence Square toward the City Hall, Sule Pagoda, and the eight-lane divided main street Sule Pagoda Road.

What we saw, and heard, was a great tragedy underway. We could hear the steady popping of rifle fire and could see many people running in all directions to get away from the shooting.

We knew that casualties were going to be heavy.

Pro-democracy demonstrators at Rangoon City Hall. Viewed from the U.S. Embassy roof-top viewing platform. This photo was taken only a few days before the army was ordered to shoot to disperse demonstrations.

A smaller group was taken under fire early in the morning on 8 August.

Ambassador Levin immediately requested an appointment with the Burmese minister of defense. The ambassador and I went together for that appointment, and to many subsequent calls during the violent months of August and September and, over time, for most of the remaining months of our assignments.

The purpose was to allay any thought that the Burmese military government might have that the U.S. military would support their actions as fellow soldiers. By having the civilian ambassador and the military defense attaché together, we made it clear that the entire U.S. government followed the same policy, and no sympathy would be forthcoming from the U.S. military leadership.

Sule Pagoda, photo taken from Embassy roof the morning of 8 August 1988. Rangoon City Hall just out of photo to the right. Large crowd at far-right center (blurred) marching on Sule Pagoda Road was taken under fire by Burmese Army while we watched, distressed and unable to help.

When we arrived at the Tatmadaw headquarters guest meeting room, we were received by the Navy chief of staff rather than the defense minister.

The ambassador delivered a firm demarche calling for the army to stop shooting unarmed civilians. The admiral responded with a chilling sentence of only eight words:

"First the people must be made to obey."

The ensuing days were dangerous. The army's indiscriminate use of deadly force against the people during the week of 8 August 1988 (known forever after as "8-8-88") and subsequent days would cause an estimated 3,000 deaths and at least as many more wounded from rifle fire.

After a week or ten days of violence a lull of two weeks ensued. Army troops and police disappeared from the streets. We wanted to know where—and why—the army and police had gone, but no answer was provided by the any Burmese government office.

The apparent end of military and police oppression caused the Burmese people to mistakenly think the lull reflected their victory over the armed forces. There began a period of increasingly large, well-organized pro-democracy demonstrations and marches throughout the city. Many of those marches passed directly in front of the American Embassy and were extremely large and well organized—several included what we estimated as well over 100,000 marchers.

One of dozens of peaceful demonstrations that passed the U.S. Embassy in August and September 1988. Some of the processions were estimated to include more than 100,000 marchers.

SNAPSHOTS

The disappearance of security forces unfortunately led to many days of deadly acts of revenge by bands of civilians armed with knives and machetes. Many suspected police informants and plain-clothed military intelligence personnel were killed. The weeks of violence and then lack of security, followed by attacks against suspected intelligence agents and undercover police officers, caused an almost total cessation of trade and business in Rangoon.

The specter of potential violence and a looming short-age of fuel and foodstuffs caused the ambassador to order all embassy family members and all but a handful of embassy officers to be evacuated to safe haven in nearby Bangkok, Thailand, until the threat of violence and short-ages passed.

The defense attaché office was directly involved in planning and carrying out the evacuation operation. The Rangoon DAO and its five personnel were awarded the Defense Meritorious Unit Awards for collective efforts to observe and report on the anti-government movement and its violent repression, and its leadership role in planning and carrying out the evacuation of most staff, all family members, as well as counterparts from many other friendly embassies in Rangoon.

The removal of police and army forces from the streets was a deliberate effort by Burmese military intelligence and security forces to determine the depth and strength of the pro-democracy movement.

On 18 September, the military junta suddenly announced a change of government and began another crackdown on the anti-government, pro-democracy activity. The ensuing violence was at least as severe as that of August, and again casualties were estimated at more than 3,000 dead and thousands more wounded by military and police activity. We were thankful that most of our staff and their families had been evacuated to safely in Bangkok.

*Armed army patrols like this filled every main intersection
in Rangoon and enforced the dusk to dawn curfew
through much of August and September 1988*

That time the military's use of violent force gained the government's objective—demonstrations ended. Thousands of mostly young people fled to the border areas for sanctuary with the plethora of anti-government ethnic insurgent groups.

An uneasy calm returned to Rangoon. A dusk to dawn curfew and increased military patrols kept the lid on widely held but now-silent anti-government feelings.

A "new normal" calm through October and November allowed family and staff who had been evacuated to Thailand to return to Rangoon.

The violence and tensions were a clear learning experience and a warning. No matter how much time I had spent learning the language, culture, and politics of Burma, that had been a surprise—and more surprises were surely to come.

My primary responsibility as the senior U.S. military officer on the embassy staff was to act as the military advisor to the ambassador.

SNAPSHOTS

I was very grateful the ambassador and I had developed an extraordinary level of professional and personal rapport.

I consider Ambassador Levin to be the finest boss, military or civilian, that I worked for during my thirty-year military career.

Another primary responsibility as defense attaché was to understand and report everything possible about, and maintain a relationship with, the host-country military. Although angered by the Tatmadaw's unrelenting violence against its people, I still needed to maintain a relationship with the host-country military leadership.

My relationships with the Tatmadaw were carried out with professionalism, and no illusions whatsoever.

My dealings with the FLO, as well as all senior Burmese officers I met, were scrupulously polite and the conversations thoroughly professional.

It was very important that official talks were delivered without emotional tone or outbursts of temper. At the same time, I used every opportunity to criticize the excesses carried out by the army against the people—that was U.S. policy as well as my personal feeling.

It was essential to be flexible and prepared for any eventuality. It was important to maintain personal and professional integrity, professional demeanor, and, yes, personal courage. I was an American soldier.

I never forgot nor forgave that incident when armed soldiers pointed rifles at me and said, "We could shoot him and claim it was an accident."

Nor did I ever forget the cold look on the face of the Navy Chief of Staff when he delivered those chilling eight words:

"First the people must be made to obey."

This stately historic building housed the American Embassy in Rangoon until 2007, when a new facility was built outside the downtown city center. This building faces Independence Square, directly across from the Rangoon City Hall.

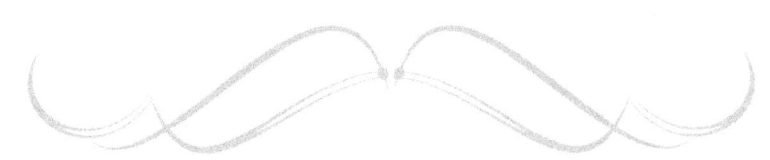

COLONEL (RETIRED) JOHN B. HASEMAN, U.S. Army, graduated from the University of Missouri ROTC Program in 1963 and served more than thirty years on active duty between June 1963 and January 1995. He spent eighteen of those years on assignments in Asia and is school trained in three Southeast Asian languages. He served twice in Vietnam. First, in the 9th Infantry Division (1967–1968), and later as a district-level advisor in the Mekong Delta (1971-1973). He became an Army Foreign Area Officer (FAO) in 1974 and spent the last twenty years of his career in FAO assignments.

He served in the Republic of Korea, Thailand, and three separate assignments in Indonesia. His final two military assignments were as U.S. Defense and Army Attaché/Senior Defense Official in Rangoon, Burma (1987-1990) and U.S. Defense and Army Attaché/Senior Defense Official in Jakarta, Indonesia (1990-1994). He holds a bachelor's degree in political science, a master's degree in public administration, and a Master of Military Art and Science degree.

Since retirement he has written extensively for publication, with five books on Southeast Asian political-military affairs, many book chapters, and more than 250 articles published in journals in the U.S., Australia, and Europe. His most recent book is *In the Mouth of the Dragon: Memoir of a District Advisor in the Mekong Delta*, 1971–1973, McFarland Publishing, September 2022.

He was inducted into the Defense Attaché Service Hall of Fame in 2011.

ARROGANCE, EGO, INTELLIGENCE

"CUSTER AND THE AMERICAN MILITARY"

Rich Vargus

W HAT HAS LED TO OUR nation's disastrous military failures? Strategy, tactics, or the arrogance and ego of military leaders? Generals driven by fame and glory believing in their general officer's tactical crystal ball rather than tactical and strategic analysis, unable to see their enemies through their rose-colored lens? This article focuses on my experience in my recent visit to the Custer Battlefield in Montana and how as a student of military history, similarities of US military failures parallel Custer's tumultuous failure at the Little Big Horn.

I've been enamored with Custer and how he and the 7th Cavalry died in glory against the savage Indians since I was a child. I watched, *They Died with their Boots On* on my black and white TV and the swashbuckling heroic Errol Flynn sacrificing the 7th Cavalry to save General Terry and Gibbon's columns from being slaughtered by Indians.

But as I continued to study tactics and read more about the truth about the Little Big Horn Campaign, it became apparent that the blunders leading to the massacre on June 25, 1876 were in no way heroic. Custer didn't sacrifice the 7th. He disobeyed his orders, violating the basic tenets of leadership and tactics. From my viewpoint and the accounts of the Indians and battlefield studies, he intentionally divided his command without any actionable intelligence, no idea of the enemy's strength, lack of terrain analysis, extending his attack formation well beyond his lines of communication and support. The tactical deadly sins.

Snap decision. Custer was a fool, letting his ego and arrogance supersede the tactical situation. Like many other senior leaders, he relied on previous wartime successes against their adversaries to deploy his meager forces.

Rule 1. Every situation needs to be assessed on its own merit. The result was Little Big Horn—Pearl Harbor of the West.

While historians have blamed Reno and Benteen for abandoning Custer, Reno's decision to retreat, even as it was in a disorganized rout, was the only sound tactical decision of the battle.

In retrospect, his retreat and selection of an effective defensive position on Reno Hill was a sound textbook tactical decision. Consolidate your forces on terrain providing the best fields of fire, cover, and concealment in a circular perimeter.

Reno Hill denied the Indians access to avenues of approach, affording the remnants of the 7th Cavalry excellent protection. The Indians, although able to surround Reno Hill, could not penetrate Reno's defensive barrier. The tactical advantage—Reno.

With every step I took on the battlefield, I became more frustrated. Even as I envisioned the fog of war, the mass confusion across the expanse of the battlefield, Troopers divided into small groups, being cut down with no hope of survival.

The terrain was the Indians back yard. It was their home. The Indians were fighting to preserve their way of life. It was their type of war, a gorilla war—an insurgency.

As I traveled across the battlefield, starting at Last Stand Hill, one could see how the Indians divided and conquered. Quickly dividing the 210 troopers and killing them off piecemeal.

Custer must have realized after he attempted an attack from the North that he had run into an Indian hornets' nest. What was he thinking? The terrain favored the Indians— the rolling hills, coulees, and deep ravines afforded the Indians the tactical advantage.

The many white headstones identifying where 7th Cavalry Troopers were killed show how easy it was for the Indians to use the cover and concealment of the tall grass and the slopping coulees. Even from Last Stand Hill, the Indians were in total control of the battlefield. Custer failed to do what he should have done, reconnoiter in force, gather intelligence, and wait for the main force to arrive.

Custer's mission was to determine enemy strength, assess the terrain, evaluate the best avenues of approach and egress, and report back to the main force. But the terrain and the village all favored the Indians. The entire village was under the canopy of the timbers. The Indians had established the locations to ford the river. The 7th Cavalry arrived blind. The Indians were able to take advantage of the vast cover and concealment. They were familiar with the terrain. They knew their avenues of approach, the river crossings.

But the *coup de grace* was Custer's arrogance and dereliction of duty in sacrificing the men under his command for the sake of glory.

Custer didn't need to attack. Regardless of his belief that if he didn't attack, the Indians would have been able to escape, the encampment was a tribal community. Women and children, teepees, were force detractors. They normally were not mounted and would have slowed any retrograde movement.

SNAPSHOTS

As we've seen across our military history, starting with Custer, the failure to understand that conventional forces in mass numbers and overwhelming firepower are not the tactical strategies to defeat a guerilla insurgency or break the will of the people.

Custer's folly, his arrogance, and ego, and failure to perform a tactical analysis of the situation reverberated across the battlefields of Little Big Horn, Pearl Harbor, Viet Nam, Iraq, and Afghanistan.

MacArthur, "The American Caesar", twice allowed his ambivalence, arrogance, and ego to overshadow the tactical situation and disregard taking a defensive posture in the Philippines at the onset of WWII. Like Custer, he knew best—his godlike decisions went unchallenged. With the attack on Pearl Harbor looming, he informed President Roosevelt he was prepared to defend the Philippines.

On December 8, 1941, the Japanese decimated his operational aircraft, leaving the Philippines wide open for unopposed Japanese landings. The massive air attacks drove MacArthur's Army into a situation where they were forced onto the Bataan Peninsula and Corregidor.

The ghost of Custer must have come back from the grave and sat on his shoulders. Underestimating the enemy, surrounded, like at Little Big Horn, cost the US any possibility of mounting a formidable defense against the Japanese, waiting for their inevitable destruction.

In Viet Nam, the Joint Chiefs of Staff and General Westmorland ignored the will of the people. The North Vietnamese waited out the Japanese and then defeated the French. How? Through their belief in nationalism and non-traditional asymmetric warfare.

The US learned nothing from the French experience in Viet Nam. Like Custer, General Westmorland's conventional strategy against an enemy who was resilient and used the jungle canopy as their domain outfoxed the conventional WWII tactical concept of the US strategy of overwhelming force.

Rather like Custer with false bravado, the US committed almost a half million troops to fight what our political leaders knew during the Eisenhower Administration was an unwinnable war. Like Custer, the French and American military ignored the people's will. The defeats at Diem Bien Phu by the French in 1954 were repeated by the shear resilience of the North Vietnamese people circumventing the jungles and mountains to bring the TET Offensive to the south and lay siege in 1968 at the Marine Base in Khe Sahn.

Unlike the Little Big Horn and Diem Bien Phu, Khe Sahn did not fall because of the overwhelming round-the-clock US air support. The US Intelligence community did not know about the North Vietnamese build-up and strength around the base. But then again, neither did Custer or the French. The siege was a total surprise to the Marines, whose defense of their Alamo was a life-and-death struggle, costing 703 killed and 2,642 wounded. Custer, 217 were killed, plus fifty-three from Reno's command, 4,020 were killed, and 9,118 wounded at Diem Bien Phu.

History repeating itself. One critical tactical flaw—we established boundaries that restricted pursuit into enemy sanctuaries. In the aftermath of the Little Big Horn, the Indians escaped to Canada. In the Southwest, they escaped into Mexico. Limited conflicts can never achieve total victory if we restrict the ability to wage total war and attack the enemy across protected boundaries.

Sitting Bull was a master strategist relying on the border to protect his people. The same strategy was successfully used by the North Vietnamese leaping into Cambodia and Laos, safe to resupply, train and re-enter the south at will, their logistical bases safe from attack. Similarly, Osama Bin Laden and the Taliban jumped into neighboring Pakistan.

SNAPSHOTS

Arrogance and ego were Custer's shortfalls. The Indians were not defeated by overwhelming military superiority. They were defeated by Manifest Destiny and American Nationalism. The American expansion to the Pacific, fueled by a continual flow of expansionists, immigrants, cattle barons, and the promises of gold, was a sea of humanity overwhelming the Indians' tribal way of life. Second, the US government engaged in a systematic purge of the Indian nations. The Indians' sheer numbers were decimated, and their light cavalry and mobility became ineffective. But the eradication of their natural food supply, the buffalo, caused starvation and disease, destroying more casualties than inflicted on the battlefield. Their population never recovered.

The imbalance of technology—repeating rifles, Gatling guns, and improved artillery against the traditional Indian bows and arrows—eventually was no match for the nomadic tribes. Yet regardless of the never-ending tidal wave of people invading their lands, the Indians' tactics of guerilla warfare and small unit tactics fought the US Army to a standstill for almost fifty years. From just before the Civil War to the end of the 19th Century.

Why?

The will of the people. Nationalism.

In Viet Nam, the ill-equipped armies of North Viet Nam and in Afghanistan, the Taliban were underestimated. The US envisioned a rag-tag band of inferior peasants easily defeated by the might of overwhelming forces. Just like Custer did at the Little Big Horn. But as the enemy in Black pajamas, our enemies in traditional tribal garb in Iraq, Afghanistan, and the Indians of the West proved the arrogant assumptions that warfighting against unconventional asymmetric forces might need to be fought with a similar strategy. That superior mindset cost Custer and countless others their lives in our nation's follies.

238

We followed the same trend in Afghanistan. The British and the Russians invaded Afghanistan to bring civilization to the region and establish a political footprint. The same never-ending failures in an attempt to defeat a tribal enemy and change their tribal culture failed. With the might of these superpowers, well-equipped, well-disciplined conventional armies failed to meet military objectives, fighting to a stalemate. The barbaric religion dominated sharia law local indigenous forces were victorious.

The strategy of the Indian Wars, Viet Nam and particularly in Afghanistan we were going to infuse civilization and win their hearts and minds. The objective of winning their hearts and minds was to change their culture, force them to accept western culture, and refute their well-engrained tribal culture.

But where did we lose these wars?

Simple. The US and our coalition partners lost the political and popular desire to continue the fight in each of these failed military operations.

SNAPSHOTS

As I drove through South Dakota and into Montana through the Badlands, I was in awe of the miles and miles of open land. For the life of me in 2022, as I continued my trek, the only time I saw any signs of life was when I came upon exits for the towns and villages that dotted the highway. It was unbelievable that 146 years later, the plains remain open, free from development and the Manifest Destiny invasion.

I couldn't grasp how the government determined the Indians needed to be forcibly contained and placed on reservations when thousands of miles of open land were and is still available that would have allowed the Native American Indians to continue to live their nomadic lives. Manifest Destiny or the destruction of the Native's way of life?

But we've seen Custer's failure to properly assess the enemy situation most recently occurred with the military disaster in Afghanistan. The hasty, poorly planned, and executed withdrawal from Afghanistan violated every fundamental principle of tactics.

We allowed our forces to be bottled up in Kandahar, vulnerable to Taliban mortar attacks. Standard force protection measures of employing standoff distance, a protective buffer allowing a corridor to manage and control access and direct threats from IEDs were ignored.

So-called refugees abutting the walls should have funneled into security lanes. Like Custer, what was the onsite commander thinking? Like Custer, overwhelming force allowed suicide bombers to come directly up to the wall and detonate, killing thirteen service members. Custer's ghost was again present in the failure to obtain and rely on actionable intelligence and underestimating the enemy's intentions. Was that arrogance or ego?

How can we avoid these blunders in the future? Custer's folly was an individual command decision. His failure to follow the basic rules of tactics and his ego led to his demise. The other failures—Viet Nam, Iraq, and Afghanistan, were a combination of political direction and failures of the military implementation of operational decisions based on what became a numbers game. Numerical metrics to determine the progression of success, but never failure. Pearl Harbor was acceptance and inability to believe an attack could take place on the bastion of the Pacific.

First, determine if a military operation is tenable and winnable. Politically using the military as pawns in a game of power is negligence. Present military commanders with a direction of winning, not a stalemate.

Military leaders rely on the situation of the current generation. Don't use strategies from the last war. The key is that war was in the past. Don't use numbers and metrics to be your measure of success. Statistics don't win battles.

Set timelines. Allow military commanders to project a winning strategy. If that fails, don't project the conflict ad infinitum. Commanders need to verify and not ignore intelligence and never assume. We can never have another unnecessary loss of young men and women as we did when we abandoned Afghanistan.

Good leaders make good decisions. Our nation has certainly trained and developed our senior leaders, who continue to lead our military. We must be cognizant of our failures and vow never to allow arrogance and ego to be part of a leadership decision.

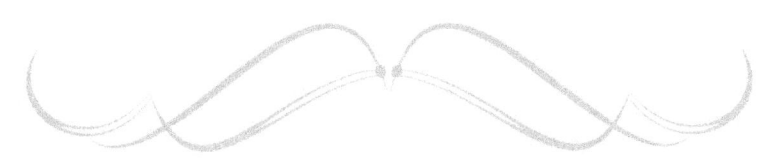

D R. (COL) RICH VARGUS INITIALLY retired in 1995 after twenty-four years of service in the United States Marine Corps and United States Army. Following retirement, he began an extended career in law enforcement.

In 2005, he was recalled to active duty, deploying to Iraq, Afghanistan, and serving at US Central Command as the chief of law enforcement. In 2012, Colonel Vargus was released from active duty. He entered federal civilian service as the Department of the Army Canine Program Manager, and in 2018 assumed the position of Department of Defense Canine Program Manager—a position he held until his retirement in April 2020.

Dr. Vargus is a recognized global leader in law enforcement serving on NATO, and European Union counter explosive canine panels and boards.

He is a graduate of the Army Command and General Staff, Air War College, George Washington University National Senior Leadership Counsel and National Security Management Course. He holds a master's degree in national defense studies and a doctorate in public administration.

MAYBE ONE DAY

Tanya R. Whitney

SITTING AT A TABLE, HIDDEN in the far recesses of an old-fashioned diner, you wait for your food. You can see the area of the dining room, but they can't see you. It's a safe space from the unknown. Your body is home, but the mind swings back and forth between home and the battlefield. Maybe one day they'll be in the same place all at the same time.

It's still difficult to function in this world, never knowing what may trigger a return to the bad place. It doesn't take much to bring back the memories and transport you back to the days of being constantly on guard. One time it was the constant popping of fireworks that had you cowering in the corner of your bedroom. Another time, a tire blew out and had you dropping to the ground in a store parking lot. The whistle of a siren or the stench of something burning is enough to cause flashbacks.

Never knowing how people will react to your strange and erratic behavior adds to the fear. The worst is when it's family and friends acting as though they don't know who you are. Their strange looks and avoidance make you feel like a leper in ancient times, so you hide every chance you get, whether in public or in private.

It is said that time heals all wounds. In your case, time only makes the wounds fester worse than an infected pustule.

SNAPSHOTS

You stare at the pair of hands flattened against the cool tile of the diner's table. Fingers are spread wide like the teacher made you do in school to make a turkey drawing. It's the only way to keep them from shaking as you wait. The nails are bitten down to the core. The cuticles are ripped away from the skin surrounding the nail bed—a sign of the constant uneasiness that filters through the body.

The backs of the hands are brown, permanently tanned by the desert sun. In stark contrast, scars whitened by time stick out. They crisscross a path from the knuckles to the wrist. Some trail up the forearm where your uniform had pulled away. Reminders of the shrapnel and debris marking them as the body reacted in fear to the attack.

Hands and arms took the brunt of the damage as they covered and protected the face and head. Gazing at the scars, the memory of how they came about infiltrates your psyche. You can't stop the visions as they run rampant, pin-balling off the lobes of your brain. The only hope before they take over is that no one will see you make a fool of yourself.

Peering through the fog of mental images of that day, you see the fingers curl inward. The voices and noises of the diner become the sounds of the mess hall located thousands of miles away in the desert sands. Fists become clenched so tightly that blood pops the veins up through the skin. The tension is reflected in the whitening of the knuckles as the hair stands on end. It's too late to stop the memories—to stop the takeover of the unforgettable images.

The body now joins in the fray. Sitting upright, it is taut with terror. You are immobilized in the slat back chair, feet glued flat to the floor. Unable to move, the heart pounds at a rapid tempo like a tympani drum. The lungs scream for air as the chest rises and falls harmoniously with the heart.

Can't get enough air. I need to get out of here.

The head is now immersed in the depths of panic. The throat is dry. Eyes are widened in confusion as the mind battles, fight or flight. The mouth gapes open and closed, trying to make a sound. There's only silence. The nose smells the odor of fire and smoke.

Or is that something burning in the diner's kitchen?

A loud bang completes the transitions. The senses have fully enveloped you in the past now. The only sights, sounds, and feelings now are of that fateful day.

The pounding of rockets and shells deafens the ears. Ears once alert to any strange sound are now muffled by the violence. They hear someone yell to get down, to get on the floor.

At least that's what you think you heard. Are you a coward for doing as they say? Shouldn't you be challenging the infiltrators? Fight or flight?

You feel a tug on your sleeve.

The mind takes over in the absence of consciousness. It reacts as trained to do for so many years. You quickly scramble under to the floor, comforted by the fact that others are there. If you're a coward, then so are they.

As you bring your arms up to protect yourself, you mentally repeat every prayer you learned in your Catholic upbringing. You try to scoot under a table, but there's no room. The debris rains down, falling like leaves from the trees in a hurricane. The sting of it hitting your skin reminds you of the time you got stung by a nest of hornets. The smell of burning flesh permeates the air around you. It is a smell that stays with you forever.

You can't tell when the shelling stops. Your ears are still clogged with the reverberation of the explosions.

Or is that the hammering of your heart?

SNAPSHOTS

The soldier next to you taps on your shoulder. Pulling your hands down, you look at him in question. He points to the blood now flowing from the veins in your hands. Hands pockmarked with the evidence of your flight to safety.

He asks if you are okay. A silent nod signals yes, but deep down you know you'll never be okay again.

The memory gradually fades back into the past. The visions and echoes are replaced with the sights and sounds of the diner. The mind registers you are away from danger. The fog in your eyes begins to clear, bringing into detail the *décor* of the roadside diner. The sounds of explosions are replaced by the melodic voices coming from the jukebox.

The mouth is closed as it swallows saliva to wet your throat. Sweat rolls down from your forehead in giant beads. The water sizzles on the heated skin as though you are in a sauna, cleansing and soothing the muscles and joints from the tension of the flashback.

Luckily, you rode the wave of the blast from the past sitting in the chair. A glance around the diner indicates no one saw your embarrassing trip down memory lane. You look down at the pair of hands on the table. No longer clenched in fear, the fingers are relaxed, curled in their natural state.

Forcing them flat against the tabletop, you stare again at the scars. The scars you feel daily are a sign of your cowardice in hiding instead of fighting. Doesn't matter in your mind that others also hovered in fear around you that day.

Maybe one day you'll believe the counselors when they say, "You are not a coward."

Maybe one day you can look back on that day and not see the dead fellow soldiers scattered around the mess hall. Maybe one day, you'll believe the scars represent your response to your years of training.

Maybe one day.

Maybe.

T ANYA R. WHITNEY RETIRED FROM the United States Army in 2010 as a master sergeant after serving over twenty-seven years. Originally from Sorrento, Louisiana, she began writing poetry a few years ago as part of her PTSD therapy. Her poetry primarily deals with her military service, but she has also written other pieces.

In 2018, she was selected as a gold medal winner for the National Veterans Creative Arts Festival in the creative writing poetry category. She has won several poetry competitions and has had individual poems published. She has also had several short stories accepted for publication.

Along with her published poetry book, *A Soldier's Journey Home*, she has individual poems and short stories published in several anthologies, including *Reach of Song 2020*, *Treasures Found in a Cedar Chest*, *Sandcutters*, *Ink to Paper Volumes*, *Southern Treasures*, and *Tears O'er a Tin Cup*.

THE BATTLE OF EUTAW SPRINGS

Salina B. Baker

AFTER THE BATTLE OF MONMOUTH on June 28, 1778, the American Revolutionary War lulled in the North where British General Sir Henry Clinton was stationed with a large part of his army in New York. King George III and the British Parliament turned their eyes on the American South and sent their armies where a civil war raged between Loyalists, those loyal to the crown, and Patriots.

In response, the Continental Congress, the American civilian governing body, sent General Robert Howe, who lost Savannah, Georgia to the British in 1778; General Benjamin Lincoln, who lost Charleston, South Carolina in May 1780; and then General Horatio Gates, who was defeated at Camden, South Carolina in August 1780. Gates shamefully left his decimated and vanquished troops and supplies behind and rode 180 miles to Hillsboro, North Carolina.

Congress' previous choices to command the Southern army had failed. Now, they left the choice to General George Washington. He chose his ablest major general: Nathanael Greene.

Nathanael found the remnants of the Southern army on December 2, 1780, in Charlotte, North Carolina. He wrote to his wife Caty, who was at home in their native state of Rhode Island,

SNAPSHOTS

I arrived here the 2d of this month and have been in search of the Army I am to command, but without much success, having found nothing but a few, half-starved soldiers who are remarkable for nothing but poverty and distress.

With little support or funding from the impoverished and disorganized Continental Congress and a countryside stripped bare of sustenance for humans and horses alike, Nathanael's little ragged and hungry army, with help from local militia, wore down the numerically superior British army in the South commanded by General Lord Charles Cornwallis.

General Nathanael Greene, painting by Charles Willson Peale from life, 1783. Author image rights ©Alamy Ltd.

From the beginning, Nathanael ignored every military doctrine that warned about dividing an army in the face of a superior foe. He detached General Daniel Morgan and ordered him to march to northwest South Carolina to protect the inhabitants and distract the British. Cornwallis sent a force of 1,000 men to stop Morgan, where they clashed on the undulating fields of a place called The Cowpens. The Battle of Cowpens, fought on January 17, 1781 resulted in a brilliant patriot defense and victory.

The loss at Cowpens infuriated General Cornwallis. After months of chasing Nathanael's army, which lost every engagement except Cowpens, an exasperated Cornwallis abandoned Georgia and the Carolinas and retreated with his exhausted and starving army into Virginia.

Then, Nathanael systematically destroyed the British outposts, supply lines, and communication lines between the British holding Savannah and Charleston and the rest of South Carolina.

Malaria, fatigue, and want of provisions took their toll on the Southern army. Nathanael led them to a camp of repose in the High Hills of Santee near Camden, South Carolina. In late August 1781, he learned that British Colonel Alexander Stewart was moving through central South Carolina, and he intended to put a stop to it. On August 23, he marched his army out of the High Hills looking for a fight.

On September 7, after weeks of mucking through swamps and heavy rains, the Southern army arrived at Burdell's Plantation, seven miles from Eutaw Springs, South Carolina, where Stewart was camped with 1,500 men. During their march, Nathanael's army picked up militia under Generals Francis Marion, Andrew Pickens, and Colonel Francois de Malmedy. Cavalry Colonel William Washington of the 3rd Continental Dragoons also reunited with them, swelling the army to nearly 2,400 men.

Nathanael ordered his troops to cook one day's provisions and allowed them a gill of rum. They would attack in the morning.

On September 8, 1781, just before dawn, Nathanael's army marched toward the enemy. At 7:00 A.M., they saw the white tents of the British Army near a brick mansion. Behind the mansion, springs drained into Eutaw Creek, which flowed into the Santee River. A British foraging party was rooting for sweet potatoes when the American vanguard spotted them.

SNAPSHOTS

Stewart sent cavalry Major John Coffin with a forward detachment. They skirmished with Colonel "Light-Horse" Harry Lee's legion.

Colonel Otho Holland Williams ordered the Patriots to, "move in the order of battle and halt."

The order of battle was familiar. It was the same deployment Daniel Morgan had executed at the Battle of Cowpens—militia up front, with orders to fire and fall back. That placed the militiamen from North Carolina and South Carolina in front with Colonel Harry Lee's legion and reinforcements from Francis Marion and Andrew Pickens.

Behind the militia, Continentals, men from Maryland, Virginia, and North Carolina, formed the line. Nathanael held Washington's cavalry and Colonel Robert Kirkwood's Delaware troops in reserve. Stewart posted a single main line of defense to the west. His 63rd and 64th Regiments of Foot looked directly across at Francis Marion.

Stewart's 3rd Regiment of Foot held the right of his line. His center was anchored with Loyalist brigades from New York and New Jersey. Musket fire exploded from both sides of the line. Continental 2lb grasshoppers boomed. The Virginia and Maryland regiments drove toward the brick mansion in a race to get inside before the British. The British won shouldering the door closed against the Americans pushing from the other side. American troops surged through the British camp and tripped over tent ropes and stakes. British marksmen opened fire. The Patriots attempted to dislodge the British with unsuccessful cannon fire.

Major John Marjoribanks tried to hold the British right flank. Nathanael ordered Colonel William Washington to push against Marjoribanks. The British in the mansion raked Washington and his dragoons. Washington's horse was shot out from underneath him. He was bayonetted and taken prisoner. Colonel John Eager Howard of Maryland was shot in the collarbone. Colonel Richard Campbell of Virginia was mortally shot in the chest. Harry Lee's deputy executed an unsuccessful charge. Nathanael's army suffered debilitating losses, and his men were scattered across the field.

After four hours of fighting, he called a retreat and rallied his bloodied, exhausted forces in the woods. Losses that day totaled a staggering 1,400 killed, wounded, missing, and taken prisoner.

Both sides claimed victory.

Eutaw Springs Battlefield in Eutaw Springs, South Carolina.
Most of the battlefield has been swallowed by man-made
Lake Marion. Photo circa 2019 by Salina B Baker

After destroying their firearms, Stewart retreated toward Charleston. Nathanael's army returned to the High Hills of Santee.

SNAPSHOTS

The Battle of Eutaw Springs was the last significant land battle of the Revolutionary War. Nathanael praised his soldiers and the militia to Congress. He was awarded a Congressional Gold Medal of Honor bearing his likeness. Otho Holland Williams was awarded a sword.

A month after the battle, due to Major General Nathanael Greene and his army's perseverance and sacrifice, the British general he had chased out of the Carolinas, Lord Charles Cornwallis, surrendered to Franco/American forces under General George Washington at Yorktown, Virginia on October 19, 1781.

That was the catalyst that ended the Revolutionary War in a Patriot victory two years later.

Daughters of the American Revolution Eutaw Springs battlefield marker. Photo by Salina B Baker circa 2019

Eutaw Springs, a poem by Philip Freneau (1752–1832). First published in the Freeman's Journal, November 21, 1781.

AT Eutaw Springs the valiant died

Their limbs with dust are covered o'er—

Weep on, ye springs, your tearful tide;

How many heroes are no more!

RESOURCES:

Beakes, John H. Jr. Otho Holland Williams in *The American Revolution*. Charleston, South Carolina: The Nautical and Aviation Publishing Co. of America, 2015.

Beakes, John H. Jr. and Piecuch, Jim. *Cool Deliberate Courage: John Eager Howard in the American Revolution*. Heritage Books, 2009.

Buchannan, John. *The Road to Charleston*. *Charlottesville*: University of Virginia Press, 2019.

Carbone, Gerald M. Nathanael Greene *A Biography of the American Revolution*, 2008.

Golway, Terry. *Washington's General Nathanael Greene and the Triumph of the American Revolution*. New York: Henry Holt and Company.

Greene, George Washington. *The Life of Nathanael Greene, Major General in the Army of the Revolution.*3 Volumes. New York: Hurd and Houghton. Cambridge: Riverside Press, 1871.

Thayer, Theodore. *Nathanael Greene Strategist of the American Revolution*. New York: Twayne Publishers, 1960.

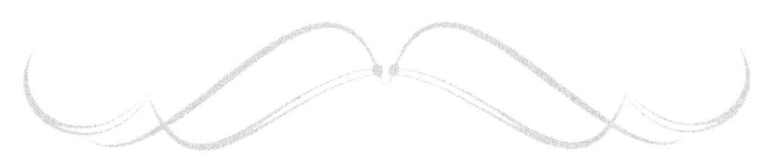

SALINA BAKER IS THE AUTHOR of a multiple award-winning adult historical fantasy series about the American Revolution called *Angels and Patriots*. Her extensive travels follow the footsteps of the compelling historical people, places, and events she passionately writes about and brings to life.

She is currently writing a novel about American Revolutionary War General Nathanael Greene titled *The Line of Splendor*.

Her ties to the U.S. Military are her grandfather U.S. Navy WWII, father U.S. Army, husband U.S. Air Force, and son-in-law U.S. Coast Guard (active duty).

Salina holds a degree in computer science. She lives in Austin, Texas.

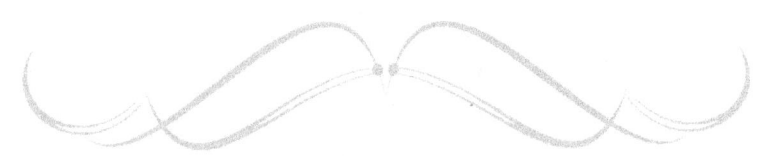

TURTLES

Michael Lund

"PICK A CARD, ANY CARD," SAID Raymond, sitting on the Winston's front porch when Mark and Cathy approached the house. The wandering veteran/would-be magician must have been waiting for the Nelsons to return from the town meeting.

"I'm not doing that," said Mark irritably. "We've had enough tricks for one day."

Like many, he'd been pleased to learn that there was a face to the Staffordshire past, but Jermaine Watt's announcement, he feared, had only slowed and not stalled the No Bridge forces. The newcomer's claim to be a figure in the town's history must be validated. And the council clearly seemed in league with Progress Industries, bringing them into the debate as if they'd been on the program.

Cathy frowned at Mark and said in a little girl's voice to the Conjuror, "Oh, I'll pick, please let me pick."

He spread the deck of cards out in a fan shape, their backs to her.

She dramatically reached her arm out and twirled her fingers like... well, like a magician's lovely assistant. She pulled one out without looking at it.

"Do I look at it, keep it," she asked, "or give it back to you?"

SNAPSHOTS

Raymond hesitated. "Well, it was supposed to go into your pocket, but it appears you don't have any."

Cathy smiled, took a light curtsy, and said again in her innocent girl's voice, "I'll just put it away right here." She slipped it into the front of her blouse.

Raymond grinned and shuffled the cards in a flamboyant manner.

Mark was going to step around him and go into the house, but Cathy put a hand on his arm to stop him.

"Be polite, dear. We have entertainment on our doorstep and should be grateful."

He stopped but pouted, nonetheless. He was concerned that the townspeople were being…well, not railroaded in this case, but perhaps channeled into a project they didn't support. At the same time, he felt the pull to take a more active role in the debate he had resisted so far.

"While you wait for me to identify the card in your beautiful wife's…um, possession, sir," continued Raymond, "let me ask you a question. How did the turtle cross the road?"

"I thought the question was 'why' did he cross the road."

Raymond dismissed that idea with a roll of his eyes. "We already know that. He wanted to get to the other side."

Mark groaned and sat down on the porch bench. "In that case, I don't know—on roller skates?"

Raymond dismissed that answer with another roll of his eyes. He turned to Cathy, whose hand was resting on the trick card's resting place, for insight into turtle behavior.

* * *

Red Bellied Turtles were common in that part of the state, large (as much as a foot long), brown or black with orange and red markings. They liked to bask in the sun on logs or stumps sticking out of shallow water, as many as four or five lined up on a single log. Some said they're Staffordshire's informal mascot because time moved slowly in that backwater village.

Red Bellied Turtles like to bask in the sun on logs or stumps sticking out of shallow water, as many as six or seven lined up on a single log.(Photo by the author.)

Cathy gave her answer to the riddle. "One foot after the other after the other after the other?"

"Ha!" Raymond chuckled. "I like it. But the answer is, 'Very, very slowly,' which your husband, a veteran like me, should have guessed."

Cathy opened her eyes wide at Mark. What did he know?

Mark shrugged. "A turtle was your replacement when you were in Vietnam—too slow getting there."

* * *

After the initial buildup of troops in Southeast Asia, in which entire units deployed from the States, many replacements came one at a time. Each had a Military Occupational Speciality (M.O.S.) and were assigned to an appropriate company in-country. They had to send a letter to let friends and loved ones back home know where they were and which units they had been assigned.

* * *

"That's right," agreed Raymond. "Did I ever tell you I had three turtles?"

SNAPSHOTS

"No," said Cathy. "But we'd like to hear."

Mark didn't know why she was indulging Ray. He did seem in a good mood, and there was no sign he'd been drinking. Still, he was likely on his way to Buzz-Buy convenience store, the Persimmon Tree Tap House, or a relative somewhere in town who would humor him. So, Mark thought the sooner he finished his card trick, the sooner they would be free of him.

The Conjuror continued to shuffle the cards as he spoke, fanning them wide, making them cascade from one hand to the other, mimicking an accordion as it expanded and contracted.

"Well, the first guy might have been nineteen years old, a farm kid from Iowa or somewhere who had no idea what he was in for. You know what I mean?"

Mark nodded.

"So, Yours Truly, Raymond, was out at some firebase where we couldn't get choppers in or out, and Turtle I was stuck back at base in Pleiku. By the time I got out, he'd seen and heard enough, so he punched out a lieutenant to land himself in the stockade."

"Could we learn which card Cathy has pulled from the pick?" asked Mark.

"Not while there are pennies falling from heaven," insisted Raymond as coins slipped from his sleeves to bounce across the wooden porch floor.

"Oh, good grief!" Mark exclaimed.

Cathy squealed with pleasure.

*　*　*

At the same time, Mark recalled the man for whom he'd been a turtle and the fact that he himself had none. When he arrived in Long Binh, the Army correspondents he joined explained that they had lost a man covering the incursion into Cambodia authorized by President Richard Nixon. So, the Pentagon had shipped him over to be Corporal Brook's replacement.

* * *

"A little help here," said Raymond, scooting some of the coins with his foot toward Mark, who was still sitting on the bench. "If I get the card wrong, you can keep all the pennies you gather."

Mark grimaced. "They're pennies, Ray."

Cathy shushed him and brushed some toward him with her foot.

* * *

Despite the relentless bombing along the Ho Chi Minh Trail, the jungle supply route from North into South Vietnam, enemy troops remained capable of mounting attacks in much of the area where American troops were stationed. Especially on the country's western border, they struck and then slipped back into Cambodia—off limits to the US military.

In April 1970, Nixon sent ground troops protected by air power to destroy North Vietnamese and Viet Cong units operating from Cambodia, claiming he was not invading a foreign country but pursuing terrorists who'd attempted to harm American citizens. They inflicted heavy casualties, captured large stores of supplies, and took prisoners. US military leaders saw this as a key step toward the end of the war.

* * *

"My second turtle made it all the way to my unit, but in the meantime, the lieutenant and I had a bit of disagreement about going into a tunnel..." Raymond's voice trailed off. He seemed to forget where his story was going.

Mark explained to Cathy. "The Viet Cong had extensive underground tunnels and complexes in the jungles—their entrances so well camouflaged that you could step right on top of them and not know they were there. We lost so many men sending them down into those hideaways that most officers decided the risk was too great to continue the practice."

Ray startled. "But not fresh-out-of-college Lieutenant Peachfuzz. So, I was spending some time back at the base when Turtle II arrived, and another guy in my unit was sent home in my place. I got to spend another thirty days in hell."

Now Cathy wanted Ray to focus on the present day and the current trick. "So, what's my card, my fellow magician?"

Ray smiled and scanned the cards. "The queen of turtles. Lovely."

Cathy pulled out the card and inspected it. It was the queen, and, looking closely, she saw a tiny image of the famous Staffordshire turtle instead of a heart, club, diamond, or spade.

"But," continued Raymond, "there's more to this trick than you think. This turtle," he turned another card around to face them, "is the knave of clubs."

"Not the jack?" asked Mark.

"The term 'knave' is clearer. It means humble servant. More to the point today, my friend," he said to Mark, "You are this knave's turtle."

"Excuse me?"

"It's time for you to step up as a replacement for Mayor Major's assistant in the fight to stop the No Bridge Cavaliers..."

"I didn't know he had an assistant."

"He doesn't. That's why it's urgent."

SNAPSHOTS

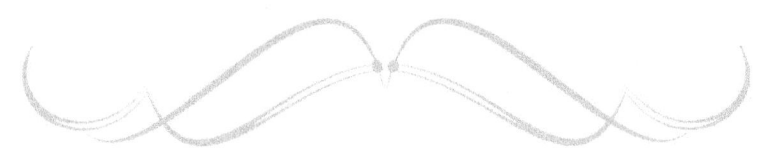

MICHAEL LUND IS A NATIVE of Rolla, Missouri and directs Home and Abroad, a free writing program for military, veterans, and family at Longwood University in Virginia. He was a U.S. Army correspondent at Fort Campbell, Kentucky (1969-70) and in Vietnam (1970-71).

He is the author of *At Home and Away*, a Route 66 novel series that chronicles an American family during times of peace and war from 1915 to 2015.

He is currently developing a series of contemporary novels set in the Tidewater region or North Carolina, which is the inspiration for Turtles.

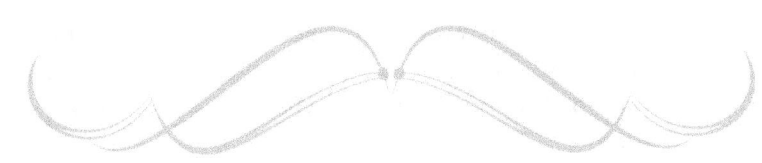

TRACES

Terry A. Williamson

YOU WILL SUFFER ALONE WHEN no one else is looking. When the battle rattle has long faded and when no one cares. An involuntary jerk and flicker of embarrassment might mark its passing.

You will remember, but not in the way of the movie screen, most likely there will be little memory footage. Whatever you've experienced becomes part of the muddy recollection that's your depression, or drug and alcohol stupor, or unfathomable malaise that nags at your soul.

There will be no one you can talk to, or cry with, because no one really gives a shit, except maybe your spouse, and she'll give up in frustration. These moments occur in silence, with no mournful taps to mark their passing. They may come at odd times, during a sad movie or a glimpse of a photograph. They can be triggered by songs, by colors, by virtually any kind of stimulus, often leaving behind a dry sob.

It is the unbridled sorrow of a lost buddy, a shattered body, or even the lingering memory of barracks chatter. If women or boyfriends don't understand, we don't really want them to. It's our anguish, our sorrow, and it's a way we can honor the dead who once shared in our comradeship.

SNAPSHOTS

Those close to you will know something is amiss, but they can't put their finger on it, nor really can you. It can be treated, but we all must suffer alone, a cloak over our emotions.

Suffering might pass, or it might not, but unlike physical wounds, it won't scar over; it remains a scab.

T ERRY A. WILLIAMSON HAS BEEN a newspaper reporter and editor, a gubernatorial speechwriter, and a communications executive.

A Vietnam veteran who served as a Marine infantry officer, he currently resides in Florida and is writing a novel on PTSD.

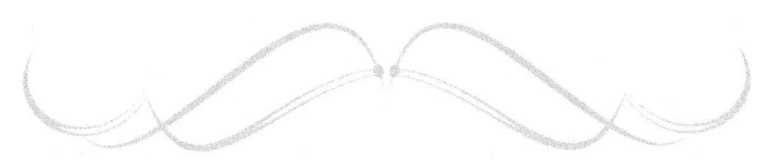

WHO NEEDS BINOCULARS?

Richard Ed Wooten, LTC, US
Army (Retired) Circa 1973

Other than Colonel Viney, names have been changed to protect the innocent and the not so innocent.

AS A NEW SECOND LIEUTENANT assigned to the 3rd Battalion, 319th Field Artillery, 101st Airborne Division, Fort Campbell, KY, my official job title was Target Acquisition Platoon Leader. All field artillery lieutenants, however, had additional duties of forward observer. Some lieutenants were assigned forward observer positions, but all lieutenants were expected to perform in that role if required.

At that time, a forward observer team consisted of an officer (usually a 2LT or 1LT), an NCO (usually a SGT or SSG), and an enlisted driver/radio operator. In 1973, the 101st was rebuilding from its service in Vietnam, so the NCO for a forward observer team was often a Spec 4 instead of an NCO.

The forward observer usually traveled with an infantry company or platoon and was responsible for calling in artillery fire in support of the infantry's mission. On some occasions, the forward observer would be assigned to an observation post (OP) where they were dug in and called in artillery fire in support of the mission of a battalion or brigade. While in an OP, the forward observer was responsible for calling in artillery fire on enemy personnel, vehicles, or equipment. In a way it was like being a sniper but with larger caliber weapons.

At Fort Campbell, OPs were assigned around the impact area where live artillery rounds, helicopter rounds, mortars, Air Force bombs, and other ordnance were allowed to be fired. The impact area was a restricted area and closed to any type of traffic because live fire could be conducted at any time and there was the possibility of unexploded ordnance (i.e., duds) being in the area. The impact area was clearly marked with various barriers and DO NOT ENTER signs.

In order to provide live fire opportunities to field artillery and aviation units, the impact areas had shells or hulls of disposed vehicles—trucks, *Jeeps*, Conex containers, etc. that could be used for targets or reference points. Most of the disposed vehicles had found their way to the impact area via *Chinook* helicopters or Air Force aircraft that dropped them there. The helicopters and aircraft never landed in the impact area.

During live fire exercise, field artillery forward observers were assigned to various OPs and called in artillery fire for their respective firing batteries (an artillery battery is a company-sized unit). The 3/319th Field Artillery had three firing batteries—Alpha, Bravo, and Charlie.

Forward observers chose a target within their assigned sectors and within their view while using binoculars. Artillery binoculars had longitudinal and latitudinal hash marks inside the lenses to assist the user in determining distances. The goal was to hit the target (or be within fifty meters of it) with the minimum number of rounds fired. That goal was accomplished by bracketing the target— firing one round over the target, adjusting to fire one under the target, and simultaneously adjusting the rounds left or right of the target. One gun fired rounds until the forward observer (through adjustment of fire commands) was confident that one gun's rounds were within the fifty-meter radius. When that was achieved, the forward observer called for "fire for effect" in which all six guns (*Howitzers*) fired one or two volleys, depending on the mission.

Most fire-for-effect missions were battery two, fire for effect, which meant twelve rounds were fired on the target. With six howitzers firing, the probability was great that at least one round would destroy the target.

Each firing battery was assigned to a specific infantry battalion for support with specific forward observers assigned to each battery. If the infantry unit wasn't deployed, forward observers were used in support of all batteries and called in fire on targets within their assigned OP.

OP 41 was my favorite OP. It was located within a mile of the eastern border of the post near a little town of Lafayette. Lafayette was a little town that looked like it had survived a time warp. It had a little general store that sold bologna, ham, and roast beef by the slice and even sold bread by the slice.

It was not uncommon for the forward observer team to take a detour off post, buy sandwiches and sodas, and then set up at OP 41 to conduct fire missions. It was like a picnic with really big fireworks.

While at an OP, the forward observer team was expected to camouflage their position and stay concealed. In reality, especially when the mission was to just provide support to the gun crews in fire missions and let the guns fire live rounds, the team lay out in the sun, drank sodas, and ate sandwiches with little regard for camouflage and concealment.

There was always the possibility of a visitor or evaluator visiting the OP, so the team always did a minimum of camouflage and concealment.

SNAPSHOTS

Our battalion also created code words to pass along on the radios so our fire direction centers (the staff who relayed our requests for fire and/or adjustment commands to the guns) would know we had a visitor or evaluator on-site.

Condition "Red Dog" meant the visitor was the battalion commander or a lesser field grade officer. Condition "Red Fox" meant the visitor was a colonel or above.

In the latter part of 1973, the division was going to have a division-wide field training exercise of five to seven days in duration.

Final preparations to deploy included signing for our weapons from the arms' room, signing for our NBC (nuclear, biological, and chemical) masks from the NBC room, and drawing any sensitive equipment such as binoculars from our unit supply room or S-4.

As we prepared to draw our binoculars, LT Taggart from Alpha Battery stated we should not draw binoculars.

He expressed his logic, "We're not going to be doing live firing. We're going to be humping the bush with the infantry, so therefore there's no need for the binos. We'll be taking the chance of damaging them or losing them. So, let's not draw them."

Sounded good and besides, LT Taggart was a first lieutenant, and we second lieutenants were accustomed to accepting the guidance/direction from first lieutenants without question.

We deployed with binoculars secured in the unit supply room.

After we deployed to the back forty acres of post, the weather very quickly took a turn for the worse. Temperatures dropped and snow began to fall.

Huah! Another great day to be a paratrooper.

Clouds closed in so all aircraft were grounded due to no visibility and the vehicle roads were reduced to mud and slush.

After two days of that misery, the division staff called an administrative halt to the exercise and ordered all troops to assemble in their respective unit's field locations and get dry and warm to prevent frostbite and/or hypothermia. Each unit had one or two medium or large type tents that had oil heaters in them, so the soldiers could dry out and get close enough to the heaters to prevent frostbite.

After a third day of that misery, the division artillery commander decided to issue live rounds to the firing battalions and to deploy the forward observers to OPs to call in live fire. His logic was that the artillery units would, in fact, be doing realistic training and the physical effort to do the training would take the soldiers' minds off being cold and might actually improve morale.

Our battalion operations officer called all the forward observer teams to the operations tent and assigned us OPs. While the live rounds were being delivered to the firing batteries, we deployed to the OPs to call in fire missions and adjust fire. Beat sitting around being wet and cold.

SNAPSHOTS

I was assigned OP 41, my favorite. My Spec 4 forward observer NCO, our driver, and I deployed. We were going to be calling in fire missions for Charlie Battery—our normally assigned battery.

When we got to OP 41, we had pretty good visibility of the close-in targets (targets within 1000 meters), but the other targets were shrouded in foggy haze and low-hanging clouds.

Binoculars would have been nice, but we just called in on the targets we could see. Besides, the real mission was to let the gun batteries stay busy and fire rounds.

As we prepared to go live, one of the other forward observer teams (for Bravo Battery) radioed to the fire direction center that they had no visibility of the impact area.

When I responded that we had sufficient visibility and targets for two teams, the other team was told to leave their current position and come join us at OP 41.

As we started our live fire missions, the fire direction center set out a radio message stating, "Forward observer teams be advised that you may encounter a Red Dog or Red Fox situation in light of brigade and division officers being in the exercise area in order to evaluate the continuance of the exercise."

"Roger that."

Seeing targets and the live rounds exploding beyond a click was extremely difficult and virtually impossible.

Again, the mission was to keep the gun batteries firing, so I resorted to John Wayne canned commands.

Those commands consisted of calling in an initial grid location for the initial command, the following commands was, "Add three hundred, left two hundred." Then, "Drop one hundred, right one hundred." Then, "Add fifty, left fifty, fire for effect."

That allowed the guns to practice adjusting elevation and other metrics on the guns. The John Wayne commands also portrayed the illusion the rounds were really bracketing the target.

Just as the second forward observer team (led by LT Taggart) joined our site, their vehicle was followed to our location by Colonel Viney, the Division Chief of Staff—a very powerful individual.

As the second team was setting up their position, COL Viney asked how we were doing. I assured him we were doing great and had just finished a couple of fire missions.

He commented on the poor visibility of the impact area and asked to borrow my binoculars.

When I told him I did not have them, he inquired, "Why?"

Thinking quickly, I explained that I was teaching my Spec 4 to adjust fire with the finger and hand method which as an approved, improvised method if binoculars were not available.

I quickly summarized how the finger and hand method worked.

COL Viney said, "Okay, now fire on that tank hull on the horizon toward the left side of the impact area."

Crap! I could barely see the silhouette of the hull but had a pretty good idea of the grid location.

I initiated the fire mission, "Fire mission, over."

"Fire mission. Send your mission, over," was the response.

"Be aware, I am under Red Fox condition, target grid location," I continued.

As we waited for the first round to be fired, COL Viney inquired, "What's a Red Fox?"

SNAPSHOTS

Showing that a second lieutenant could think on his feet, I stated, "It's an unofficial code we've adopted to mean we're firing live, but with restricted vision.

After three adjusting rounds which I claimed to see, I shouted into my radio's handset, "Flash! Fire for effect!"

"Flash" meant I had seen a bright red or yellow flash from the target indicating a direct hit.

As the fire-for-effect rounds were being readied, COL Viney questioned whether the last round had hit the target. He was adamant that he had not seen a flash.

LT Taggart, who had assumed the position of just being an observer, substantiated my comment, "Sir, I saw a yellow flash."

Before COL Viney could have me cancel the fire-for-effect command, the radio echoed, "Shot, over," which meant shots were in the air.

"Shot, out," I replied into the handset.

As the six rounds hit around the target, or at least the impact area, a red flash appeared through the haze—a round had hit the hull.

Whew.

I looked at COL Viney.

He shook his head and said, "Okay, lieutenant, I saw that one. I still question whether you really saw a flash on the previous round, but you're either lucky or good."

I did not feel a response was warranted, so I opted for silence.

As the rounds' explosions echoed across the impact area, the fire direction center informed us, "We are at cease fire. Redeploy to the battalion field location."

COL Viney continued imparting guidance. "ALWAYS have all of your equipment, especially binoculars in the future. Even if you are teaching the finger and hand method, you need a means to verify the accuracy and the binoculars would provide that means."

LT Taggart and I responded, "Yes, sir."

We exchanged salutes.

COL Viney left, and we headed back to the battalion's field location.

Needless to say, COL Viney informed the division artillery commander (another Colonel) who relayed the information to our battalion commander who was not amused.

By sunrise the next morning, we had infiltrated to the battalion rear area and secured all of our binoculars.

Huah!

SNAPSHOTS

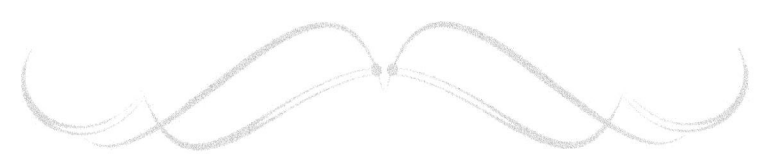

RICHARD ED WOOTEN, LTC, U.S. Army (retired) received his commission in 1971 as a second lieutenant from Clemson University as a quartermaster, detailed field artillery. He completed his field artillery detail at Fort Campbell and migrated into his commissioned field of quartermaster. (Yes, being an Airborne Ranger Quartermaster was intimidating to some.)

During his twenty-year career, he was a company commander with the 101st Airborne Division (Air Assault) at Fort Campbell, KY and was a battalion commander with the 2nd Armored Division at Fort Hood, TX.

During his career, he had two tours in Germany, with the 8th Infantry Division and 21st Support Command. His awards and decorations include Ranger tab, Senior Parachutist Badge, Department of Defense Meritorious Service Medal, and Army Meritorious Service Medal (x4).

"Aw, Tough Luck Mate…"

Joseph Tedeschi

How convoluted must one go to weave the story of a joke? Well, since the joke at the heart of this story has spare meaning without the context from which it was drawn – here's the whole story from the beginning.

Exchange Officer with the British Army

I NEED FIRST TO PLACE myself as a US army officer serving with the British army in England in 1972. To explain further, the US and Great Britain have agreed for a number of years to exchange military officer positions at various key installations and schools to enhance cooperation and better understanding between their armies.

One of my army career highlights was serving as the US army exchange officer with the British Defense Nuclear, Biological, and Chemical (DNBC) school in Salisbury, United Kingdom, located in the small village of Winterbourne Gunner, just outside of Salisbury. During the period of my exchange assignment (1970–1972), twenty-six US army officers were being exchanged with their British counterparts.

That was an exciting and challenging assignment, rewarding me with a rich and fascinating military experience and a wonderful life adventure for me, my wife, and two daughters. We made a number of new acquaintances and thoroughly enjoyed British hospitality and friendship.

SNAPSHOTS

On the military/professional side, I was fully integrated as an instructor of US Army NBC (Nuclear, Biological, Chemical) operations for all British Forces officer and NCO courses given at the DNBC school. In addition, I was assigned as Chief of Trials Division, conducting hands-on service trials of the full range of British NBC equipment.

Any misgivings I might have had about being a foreign officer serving with another nation's military were quickly dispelled. I was welcomed, and it was made known to me that I would be an essential part of the DNBC school staff.

To comply and demonstrate my full agreement with that arrangement, I modified my daily uniform by wearing US Army trousers and sporting the very comfortable British Army "wooly pulley" (sweater) as an upper garment. My officer exchange was nearly so complete and integrated that it even included being assigned secondary duties such as the Officer in Charge (OIC) of the officer's mess and the task of auditing the sergeants' mess. I readily accepted those additional opportunities to serve the DNBC school and immensely enjoyed doing them.

NBC Trials in Norway

The rewarding two-year exchange with the British army was further enhanced by participating in military activities outside the UK, such as integrating NBC equipment and operational trials with British forces conducting annual NATO training exercises in Norway. I was a member of the DNBC school trials team conducting these exercises (titled Hardfall) on two separate occasions.

The trials team traveled from the UK to Norway for several weeks each year, during which I experienced a close bond with the British army troops designated to test NBC equipment under severe winter conditions. On the second of these trips, our trials team linked with a battalion of one of the renowned British army guard units, the Scots Guards, to conduct the trials.

NORWAY EXERCISE HARDFALL 1972

Hardfall Trials Team (back to front): Flt Sgt Greenwell (Trials NCO), Nicholls (CDE PORTON), Dr. J.D. Nelms (APRE), Wg. Cdr.Hubbard (Trials Director), Mr. C. Simcock (SCRDE), Sqn Ldr Bridges (Trials Project Officer), Cpl Barker (Trials Photographer), Lt. Col J. R. Tedeschi (Trials Coordinator). The mixed leadership team included British civilian government scientific personnel, Royal Air Force regiment, and British army officers.

The battalion had just completed a security assignment in Northern Ireland and was assigned to the NATO training exercise without any in-between home leave breaks between assignments. I met the battalion commander on the train ride from Voss to Mjolfjell (the site for the trials).

He told me his troops were sorely in need of rest and recuperation from the intensive security duties they had been conducting in Northern Ireland. He was concerned for their morale.

For that reason, he had rented an entire pensione (a large winter vacation boarding house) in Mjolfjell for his officers and senior enlisted men as they had invited their wives to stay with them during the trials. That outstanding leader would have done the same for all his men had there been more facilities available. Since our trials team was also billeted at the same pensione, we became acquainted with many of them since the large edifice contained multiple rooms and a dining area for all the families to share.

*RAF Regiment Wing Commander Rod Hubbard
and author at the Mjolfjell Train Station*

THE SCOTTISH SOLDIER

Thus began my introduction to the Scottish soldier and the unique way he spoke the English language. Just after arriving at the train station in Mjolfjell, we were told we would be provided transportation to the pensione. Shortly thereafter, a pair of snowcats (treaded motorized vehicles) arrived, and the two drivers approached our assembled team. They were dressed in khaki military coveralls and black berets with no attached rank or unit insignia.

One of the drivers made a strange and, to me, unintelligible announcement to the assembled group. As he did so, I turned to Rod Hubbard, a fellow team member, and said, "It looks like they've sent us Norwegian drivers."

Bemused, Rod turned back to me and responded, "Those are not Norwegians. They're Scottish soldiers. You had better get used to the way they talk."

And for the next three weeks, I made my best effort to "get used to the way they talked" so that I might understand the language of those remarkably tough and seasoned soldiers. I spent a great amount of time up close with them during the trials. Toward the end of the trials period, I had begun to understand them just a little better. My understanding was enhanced when I realized I had to filter out the one word they used as a noun, verb, adjective, and adverb in all their conversations—the infamous f-bomb. By doing this, I could make sense of the few English-sounding words between the f-bombs to understand what they were saying.

CONDUCTING THE TRIALS

For the trials, the soldiers of the Scots Guard battalion bivouacked in tents on the frozen, snow-covered Norwegian landscape several miles away from the pensione. One of the trials called for a squad of soldiers (twelve men) to simulate being in a chemical defensive posture overnight in their squad tent. The purpose of the trial was to determine if the atropine syrettes (the antidote to nerve gas) each man carried could be prevented from freezing if the men placed the syrette under their armpits for warmth.

The trials team decided to join the men as a gesture of our appreciation and understanding for the task we were asking them to perform. Still, because of the limited space in their tent, only one of us could be with them at any time throughout the night. We drew straws to determine who would join the men, each of us doing a two-hour shift. I drew the midnight to two A.M. shift, and despite the hours, I was eager and curious to have this experience.

SNAPSHOTS

We were to take temperature readings and check the condition of the syrette that was to be placed under the armpit of the sentry posted outside the tent for an hour duration on a rotating basis. The squad sheltered under a circular tent simulating combat conditions and followed their unit SOP (standard operating procedures) for security, sleeping bag arrangement, etc.

The snowcat drove me from the pensione and dropped me off at midnight next to the squad tent at the bivouac site. I relieved the trials team member who was on site for the previous two hours and joined the squad of men already sleeping on the snow-covered ground in heavy sleeping bags.

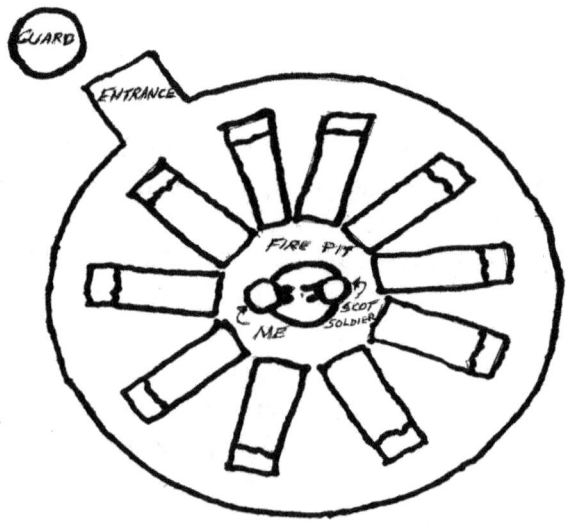

SKETCH OF SQUAD TENT

When I entered the tent, the first thing that struck me was the bayonet hanging from a wire above each of the ten sleeping bags arranged in a circular pattern on the tent floor.

I was told they hung a bayonet over each sleeping bag to cut their way out of the tent in any emergency, such as a tent fire or enemy action which might require a rapid exit. The foot of each sleeping bag came together in the middle where a fire pit had been dug in the snow.

The fire pit was wide and deep enough for one of the soldiers to sit and tend the Coleman lantern hanging from the roof of the tent (which stayed on all night) and a small camp stove at the bottom of the pit to heat water for tea.

The SOP called for one-hour shifts. Each man rotated duties which consisted of tending the lantern and camp stove (along with boiling water and the makings for tea), awakening the next soldier in line for sentry duty, and then standing guard outside for the next hour.

The soldier coming in from guard duty was given a cup of tea and then located the "warm" sleeping bag just vacated by the man going on duty.

With minimal space in the tent, the only place available for the trial team member was the fire pit, and thus I found myself sitting for two hours with two different Scottish soldiers for the duration of my shift.

I sat opposite the soldier manning the fire pit just a couple of feet apart, with our feet dangling in the pit. When I first sat down, I must confess that I had a moment of reflection as I pondered, *What the hell am I doing here and how did I end up sitting on frozen snow in the middle of a Norwegian winter night in a tent full of sleeping soldiers—with a Scottish soldier next to me trying to make conversation?*

I'm certain my Scottish soldier companions sitting next to me were thinking along the same lines—Who was this American officer "bloke," and what was he doing here sharing our discomfort? The awkward situation of sitting next to each other in the fire pit demanded that we get to know each other, and so for an hour with each soldier, we tried to converse to become acquainted.

SNAPSHOTS

THE JOKE

I could never recall all the details of our conversations or the difficulties and pauses that took place as I tried to understand what they were telling me. But I do remember they mostly talked about their recent deployment to Northern Ireland and what a tough and demanding job it had been to maintain order and peace under almost impossible political and religiously charged conditions.

The animosity between the conflicting religious factions had been fierce, and the soldiers were often called upon to make quick decisions in life-threatening situations.

The two Scottish soldiers did their best to describe to me in candid, straightforward soldier language the hostile environment in which they found themselves.

It all came together for me when one of the soldiers, describing and relating to what he had experienced, told me a joke going around within their ranks while they were there.

Now, since I have come to the point of finishing the context of the story behind the joke, I can now tell the joke (hopefully with proper respect to all parties mentioned in the joke):

An American was walking through the streets of Belfast, and from behind a corner, an arm went around his neck. The point of a knife was placed at his throat.

In a menacing whisper, the assailant asked, "Are you Catholic, or are you Protestant?"

The American had to think very fast under this threatening situation, and a flash of inspiration caused him to reply, "Well, I'm neither. I'm Jewish."

To which the assailant sneered, "Aw, tough luck, mate. You've just run into the only Arab in the IRA!"

I've cleansed the joke of all the potentially offensive nouns, verbs, adjectives, and adverbs, but I guffawed by the fire pit when I first heard it in the Scottish soldier vernacular.

I've remembered it all these years and occasionally tell the joke in the company of polite society (cleaned up version, of course). But over the years, I've realized what the joke was all about and why the soldier wanted to share it with me.

The joke contained all the elements of the stress and tensions those young soldiers faced and reflected all the contradictions and political animosity they had to endure while conducting an impossible peacekeeping mission. And, they tried to make sense of it all with a crude and improbable joke.

That young soldier may never have heard of G.K. Chesterton's take on the necessary place of humor in our lives when he said, "Humor can get in under the door while seriousness is still fumbling at the handle."

Still, he certainly proved the wisdom of that quote with his joke.

Looking back now, I realize I was the recipient of humor and hard-won wisdom sitting by that fire pit on a cold Norwegian winter night many years ago—both improbably coming to me from the mouth of a young Scottish soldier boiling water on a camp stove.

POSTSCRIPT

The overall trials period was curtailed by a few days when a blizzard was forecast. The Scots Guard battalion broke camp and returned to the pensione area as the blizzard broke in upon us (captured in the attached photo).

SNAPSHOTS

Scots Guards trekking out of the blizzard

It was an honor and a privilege to team with these Scottish soldiers, and I will always be grateful for this opportunity. During a later phase of my army career, I had another treasured military experience when I visited and spent the night at Sterling Castle in Scotland, the Home Depot for the Scots Guards.

I was part of a small US Army military delegation to the United Kingdom. We were invited to be overnight guests by the warden of Sterling Castle, a retired brigadier from the Scots Guards.

The warden and his wife gave us an intimate tour of the castle. The castle contained all the memorabilia and rich history of the Scots Guards, handsomely displayed in the great hall and throughout the rooms.

We learned that every recruit entering the Scots Guards is required to spend a period of time at the castle to absorb and appreciate the legacy of this proud military unit before reporting for active duty.

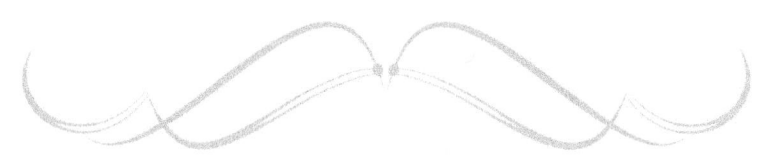

Joseph Tedeschi began his college education at St. Lawrence University in Canton, New York, before initiating his army career at West Point, graduating in 1957. Eventually earning his army-sponsored Master of Science degree in physics from Iowa State University (1963), he went on to fill army assignments in nuclear, biological, and chemical operations and materiel acquisition.

Upon retiring from military service as a regular army colonel, he worked fourteen years in the defense industry developing a counter-battery radar for three European nations.

He then transitioned to a higher calling as he entered the deaconate program in his Catholic diocese of Trenton, New Jersey, where he served for eighteen years, retiring in 2020.

MISSING IN ACTION

Carol Markowitz

IT WAS MAY 1942, SIX months after the attack on Pearl Harbor. In those six short months everything had changed. The country's antiwar isolationism was swept away by the attack and the whole country went to war. All manufacturing was dedicated to the production of supplies and materiel for the armed forces. Young men signed up everywhere and many were drafted. College students left school for the military and colleges accelerated programs— students could quickly finish their education and enlist.

Billy and Joan were high school sweethearts, graduating in 1939. When he was drafted, Joan worried about him. Like her brothers, he seemed terribly young. He was assigned to a training camp, and they began writing to each other almost every day. Billy was a twenty-three-year-old private in the U.S. Army stationed at Camp Chaffee near Fort Smith, Arkansas. Camp Chaffee was the new home of several Armored Divisions, and Billy's unit was the 93rd Armored Field Artillery Battalion.

In Billy's first letter, he sent Joan a picture.

In the picture he's sitting on a porch railing outside his barracks. He has a handsome face with dark hair and deep-set dark eyes. He has a little half smile in the picture. He is a proud newly minted soldier—his uniform freshly pressed with a jaunty tilt to his cap.

SNAPSHOTS

Joan carefully mounted the picture in her scrapbook and printed, BOY AND BARRACKS under it.

In May 1942, Joan was a junior at the New Jersey College for Women. She lived with her mother, grandmother, and two brothers in New Brunswick, New Jersey. Living close to campus, Joan walked to class every day.

Her house was painted white, like most houses on the block. It was tall and narrow, with a narrow lot. There was a tiny back yard with just enough room for a victory garden. The house sat on a little hill, and in front, two sets of steep brick steps led to the street.

Inside was a cozy living room, with a radio in one corner where the family gathered at night to listen to comedy with Bob Hope and Jerry Colonna, the music of *Your Hit Parade* or President Roosevelt's *Fireside Chats*.

At the back of the house was a large kitchen where Joan's mother baked her famous pies. There was often a pot of sauce or stew simmering on the stove. With one son in the army, Joan's mother, Francis, was happy to host dinners for soldiers stationed at nearby Camp Kilmer.

Joan's brother Jim was the oldest, and the man of the house. Tall and solidly built, he had a quick smile and a wicked sense of humor. He joined up after Pearl Harbor and was serving in a tank battalion. Francis worried about him every day. She lived through the horrors of the Great War. It felt like a very recent memory to her.

In June, Joan's classes were over, and the long summer days stretched out before her. She wrote to Billy in Fort Smith, Arkansas—a place she had never seen and could hardly imagine.

Like summers before, she worked at a children's camp nearby; her love of children led her to pursue a career in teaching. After work, she and her friends played tennis at the public courts or went into town in the evening to the soda shop or to catch a movie.

Summer turned into fall, and Joan headed back to college to finish her senior year. Billy completed basic training and became an accomplished gunner in the battalion.

He told Joan they were in combat training. They were running ten miles a day and getting used to living in the field, sleeping outside, washing, shaving, and doing laundry. He was proud of his accuracy rating on the range, and he was promoted to corporal.

As the months passed, letters flew back and forth between New Brunswick and Camp Chaffee. Billy wanted more news about Rutger's football team and, of course, more pictures. His unit became a model for the artillery, and they were reassigned to Fort Sill, Oklahoma. They were considered a training unit, giving demonstrations. But the main concern of the men was, "When will we ship out?"

As Billy put it, "When can I kick old Hitler in the pants?"

In August 1943, Joan and her mom hung a second star in the window. Her younger brother Pete joined the Navy. Just out of high school, he was headed to Rhode Island for basic training.

He wrote to Joan,

Where did you get that 'little brother' business. Don't you know I'm in the Navy? And that means I'm a man. Anyhow, that is what our commanding officer says.

At just eighteen years old, he started signing his letters, "Porthole Pete".

Billy and the 93rd got word they were shipping out. He sent Joan his new address: HQ BATTERY 93 A.F.A. NEW YORK, NEW YORK.

On August 21, 1943, the USS *Thurston* left New York harbor with the men of the 93rd settled into bunks below deck. They joined a fast convoy—their destination Oran, Algeria. Now that his letters were read by the censors, he couldn't say where they were and what they were doing but he talked about swimming in the Mediterranean, seeing "pretty French girls" and their:

> ...*open air theater. The picture may be old, and the film breaks every five minutes. Otherwise, it's okay. Yesterday, I saw* **The Major And The Minor**.

After settling in, the battalion was outfitted with a new set of combat equipment. Speed and accuracy were critical for the field artillery to successfully support the infantry, so the men spent the month of September training and getting their new equipment ready for combat.

On October 14, Billy and the 93rd boarded LSTs bound for Italy. He landed in Bagnoli on October 23rd and "was immediately greeted with its first good air raid."[1] By the end of October, they had crossed the plains of Salerno. Now attached to the Army's VI Corps, they were pursuing the Wehrmacht who were falling back to their Winter Line.

As Churchill described it,

> *In these rocky mountains, a great fortified system had been created with lavish use of concrete and steel. From their observation posts on the heights the enemy could direct their guns on all movements in the valleys below. Our troops made great effort though gaining little ground.*[2]

The 93rd were in the mountainous region south of the well-defended Mignano Gap and the route which would lead the Allies to Rome.

In early November, the 93rd was assigned to General Clarke's 5th Army. They moved north toward the Mignano Gap. They encountered steep terrain, freezing rain, and positions that were well defended by the enemy. Their attempts to capture Monte Camino and the Gap were unsuccessful. The soldiers began to call Monte Camino, Murder Mountain. The men struggled on the steep slopes carrying food and ammunition up and the wounded or dead back down.

Joan did not get any letters from Billy during the month of October, in his letter of November 1st, he said they had been busy and that he wouldn't be able to talk about what they were doing until after the war. He said he was fine and somewhere in Italy.

He asked about the Rutger's football team and said,

Boy, what I wouldn't give to see a good game. I don't remember the last one I saw.

Although Billy told her in his last letter he had not heard from her in a long time, Joan had written him several letters filled with news from home, gossip about friends, her new job, and the latest football scores. He never received them.

Billy's unit was in the heat of the battle for central Italy. The 93rd provided artillery fire for the 3rd Infantry, which was bogged down south of Mignano.

The second position was the unforgettable one at the base of Mount Fiello. It was in this position that all men learned one lesson...if the German can see you, he can get you.[3]

Now, Joan held her own letter written to him, unopened. It was stamped, RETURN TO SENDER. On the front of the envelope, Missing was printed and signed by an officer of the 93rd. Missing.

Billy's family was notified. Billy was missing from his unit, lost while they were under heavy enemy fire in the Italian mountains. The sweet funny kid who used to tease her in high school, gone. But there was hope and Joan clung to it. Maybe he was alive and was being held prisoner.

SNAPSHOTS

She shared her fears with her brother, Pete. Pete wrote back to her with all the optimism of a young sailor, still in basic training.

Too bad about Billy but don't that sound funny that you hope that he turns up a prisoner, maybe he will turn up a hero, safe and sound.

Three of her letters were returned in November and by the end of the month there had been no word.

For the 93rd, it was the deadliest month of the war. Nine soldiers of the 93rd were killed in action during the month of November, and Billy's status remained, REPORTED MISSING.

In December there was still no word. It was eerie when Joan got a Christmas card from him postmarked December 10. He had mailed it on October 9. The line drawing on the front showed Santa riding in a tank with the word, HAVOC printed on the side. The tank was surrounded by a border of holly with MERRY CHRISTMAS printed across the bottom. The card was signed with his customary close, *Yours for the Asking, Billy.*

In late December his family finally got news.

Billy had been captured and was being held in a German POW camp in Furstenberg, Prussia. Joan received a Postkarte from him in January 1944. The card was printed in pencil, sent from Stalag IIIB, PRISONER OF WAR CAMP was printed in German across the top.

He described having,

Xmas dinner with a couple of French Legionnaires. I'm getting to be quite a cook. You either have to learn or starve. Give my regards to everyone, hope to see you soon. Merry Xmas.

Camp life in winter in Germany was brutal. The men were housed in long wooden barracks. There were three-tiered rough bunks and a single wood stove for heat and cooking. The frigid wind blew through gaps in the walls. Many of the men lacked warm clothing. They lived on meager rations of thin soup, bread, jam, and "ersatz" coffee. Red cross packages containing canned goods and biscuits arrived but usually had to be shared by several men.

The POWs lost weight. Hunger and malnutrition were common throughout the camps.

The winter of 1944 wore on, wind and snow howling around the wooden barracks. The men played cards to escape the boredom. Mail delivery was the highlight, letters from home were treasured and read over and over. According to one POW they bet on everything—who had the best shoeshine or the best soap carving. Cigarettes were the currency.

In one letter Billy sent a cryptic message to Joan.

How is your brother making out? I'm counting on him.

Hoping and praying to be liberated, he was referring to Joan's brother Jim, who was serving in a tank battalion.

The long winter turned to spring and summer, with no end to the war in sight for the prisoners. Billy was receiving Joan's letters, but they were usually a few months old by the time they arrived. He wrote that they were playing baseball and soccer.

By December, he was hopeful, he may have heard some war news. Makeshift radios were hidden in some barracks, and they could receive the BBC. French troops had liberated Strasberg and the Allies were advancing toward the German border.

But he would spend another Christmas in the stalag. He wrote to Joan that he had heard the song and he knew that, he'd be home for Christmas, "only in my dreams."

SNAPSHOTS

January 1945, Soviet troops advanced through Poland and approaching the German border. Audie Murphy who was serving with the 7th Army in France wrote,

The temperature even at mid-day seldom rises above 14 degrees. Snow is almost knee deep...the nights are one long hell.[4]

It was in that hell that the prisoners in Stalag IIIB were given the order to move out. The Germans moved POWs west to escape the advancing Soviet Army. Many of the prisoners had no overcoats or boots.

They marched for seven days through deep snow and freezing cold with little food or water. Some did not survive. After marching for 108 KM, they reached Stalag IIIA at Luckenwald, just south of Berlin.

Billy wrote to Joan with his new address. He started the letter with a simple statement after the hellish week-long march,

Slight change in address. We've been moved.

Conditions in Stalag IIIA were grim. The camp was overcrowded with men who had been moved there from the east. They were living in tents in the freezing cold.

Each tent housed hundreds of men, sleeping on wooden floors with ragged blankets. Two water faucets provided water for hundreds of men, and they were nearing starvation.

Billy wrote,

I'm just dying for some flapjacks and cakes. That's all we've been thinking about.

But he believed that liberation was coming and told Joan to decide where to go on their date because,

...it won't be long, now.

On April 22, 1945, the men imprisoned at Luckenwald woke to find that their German guards had fled. They heard Soviet tanks rumbling down the road. The tanks rolled right over the barbed wire and into the camp, and the POWs stood in the compound and cheered.

The Russians did not release the prisoners right away but provided them with much needed food. Billy, survivor of the brutal fighting in Italy, the Black March through the snow in Germany and sixteen months in two POW Camps was coming home.

He wrote to Joan.

The return address said it all: CORPORAL WILLIAM FLETCHER, EX-POW, GERMANY.

NOTES:

1.   Reinertsen, Leif. *After Five: History of the 93rd Armored Field Artillery Battalion*. Germany, 1945, 17.

2.   Churchill, Winston S. *Memoirs of the Second World War: An Abridgment of the Six Volumes of the Second World War*. Boston: Houghton Mifflin, 1959, 797.

3.   Reinertsen, Leif. Op. Cit., 17.

4.   Murphy, Audie. *To Hell and Back: The Classic Memoir of World War II by America's Most Decorated Soldier*. New York: Picador, 1977, 228.

SNAPSHOTS

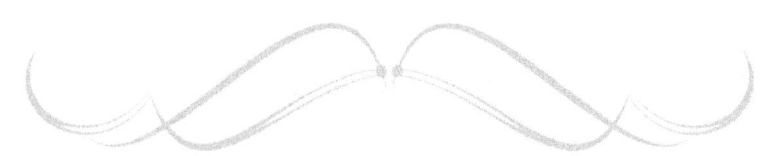

CAROL MARKOWITZ IS A RETIRED educator, having spent more than forty years providing services to children and adults with autism. She is the author of *Aging, Estate Planning, and Funding Services for Adults with Autism Spectrum Disorders*. She retired in 2016 to pursue new challenges.

When Carol discovered an extraordinary packet of letters in her late mother's belongings, she knew that she wanted to write about them. She has spent the last six years studying World War Two, focusing primarily on the war in North Africa and Europe.

Carol is a member of the Author's Guild, the U.S. Naval Institute, and the Military Writers Society of America. She writes about World War II on her blog, *Yours for the Asking*.

THE GREAT MARIANAS
TURKEY SHOOT

AIR GROUP LEADERSHIP ON DISPLAY

Ernest Snowden

M ANY YEARS INTO HIS RETIREMENT, former Chief of
Naval Operations Admiral Arleigh Burke rumi-
nated on the nature of leadership for a piece in
Proceedings magazine. After thirty-eight years in uniform
at all levels of command, including an unprecedented three
terms as Chief of Naval Operations, Burke had formed
immutable opinions on the subject:

> *...no man becomes a great leader unless he*
> *develops within himself the traits necessary to be*
> *a leader... the easiest way to find what those traits*
> *are and learn how to acquire them is by studying the*
> *leaders who have gone before.*[1]

That Burke possessed ample leadership qualities is
incontestable, but with that acknowledgment he could
have been pointing to experiences in mid-career when
he was chief of staff to the commander of Task Force 58,
Vice Admiral Marc Mitscher.

Burke reported to the senior aviator in command of
a large force of aircraft carriers that in June 1944 was
heading for a collision with a formidable Japanese fleet.

SNAPSHOTS

Nearing the third decade of the 21st century much has changed since we last competed with another naval power for control of the sea. Chief of Naval Operations Admiral John Richardson has challenged today's Navy to build on a history of service, sacrifice, and success to "create a climate of operational excellence that will keep us ready to prevail in all future challenges."[2]

Operational excellence was, in those months of war at sea in the Pacific, noteworthy for the leadership on display by commanders of individual units in the task force. Burke would have had frequent occasion to interact with and observe the leadership examples of many of his carrier air group commanders as they prepared for and directed their naval aviators in the titanic engagement to come.

In a single day of adrenaline-charged aerial combat on June 19, 1944, those American naval aviators vanquished the remaining air forces of the Imperial Japanese Navy. Then, by the end of the following day, and in concert with American submariners, they dealt a disabling blow to Japan's last great carrier fleet.

The year 2019 marks the seventy-fifth anniversary of that epic World War Two confrontation in Pacific waters west of Guam known as the Battle of the Philippine Sea. In the epic hagiography of naval aviation's first century, it is more popularly known as the Great Marianas Turkey Shoot. It became an exhibition of aerial leadership by a generation of seasoned air group commanders who had grown up in pre-war squadrons of fabric biplanes learning their organizational skills in the conduct of fleet problems.

Two air group commanders in Task Force 58 that Captain Arleigh Burke knew individually, stand out for the achievements of their commands in the Philippine Sea and the leadership examples they modeled in pursuit of those stunning accomplishments. Their commands were far and away the top-scoring air groups in that engagement.

Air Group Fifteen in USS *Essex*, on the first day of battle, scored a single day high of 68.5 enemy aircraft destroyed. Air Group Sixteen in USS *Lexington* scored a near second with forty-six enemy aircraft destroyed with no losses.

On the second day of battle, Air Group Fifteen was repositioned to defend the Saipan landing force, bringing into play its bombing and torpedo squadrons, while Air Group Sixteen's bombing and torpedo squadrons, farther to the west, contributed to sinking one enemy light carrier and delivering incapacitating wounds to another two enemy carriers.

Of note, more than half of the junior pilots in those air groups were reserve officers that had been in uniform less than three years and winged as naval aviators less than two years.

Those spectacular combat results reflect unrivaled flying skill, tactical competence, and unit discipline. Individual squadron commanders played an enormous part, however the results bespeak a noteworthy leadership talent on display by the two group commanders: Air Group Fifteen's Commander Dave McCampbell and Air Group Sixteen's Commander Ernie Snowden.

A closer look at recorded examples of their leadership in practice yields instructive insights of the sort that Admiral Burke would later reflect upon.

Much has been written in the pages of Proceedings and elsewhere on the subject of naval leadership before and since Burke's observations, in the spirit of deconstructing its essence and delivering prescriptive rule sets for its application. Ultimately, leadership becomes an expression of style that "reflects the personality of the individual."[3]

The dash and verve exemplified by those two highly confident and convivial commanders marked them quite high on the sociability register, and no doubt "had a strong influence on promoting a similar spirit of dash and verve among those who served under such a leader."[4]

Yet, most writers on the subject of leadership effectiveness, among them Ralph Stogdill in his *Handbook of Leadership*, reduce the calculus to three factors: the individual, the group, and the situation.[5]

Rear Admiral James Winnefeld, Sr., in his *Advice for Midshipmen*, cites a longer list that can be distilled to the same set of factors: the individual—be the first to get qualified, look for opportunities to educate yourself, and prepare yourself for command by developing your leadership style; the group—look out for your men and women; and, the situation—be exacting, go where the action is, lead from the front. [6]

U.S. Army Major C.A. Back, writing in *Proceedings* in 1974, lands on a similar formulation: "Know Yourself... Know Your Men... Know your Business."[7]

There is remarkable consistency among disparate writers on the subject, and the actions of McCampbell and Snowden conform closely to these precepts. Where their actions indicate strong correlation, their example provides profitable lessons in behavior for future leaders.

Know Yourself. That McCampbell and Snowden exemplified self-edification in great measure may be assumed. How they assimilated professional skills—by doing and by observing and adopting—throughout their careers merits examination.

Common experiences in uniform, often in the same command, suggest the process of personal growth began early and unfolded over several years.

Both were excellent athletes at the Naval Academy. Snowden, in the Class of 1932, was a two-year letterman in wrestling, while McCampbell finished with the Class of 1933 as a champion diver. Both acknowledged their athleticism contributed greatly to the spatial orientation and coordination that made their superb airmanship second nature.

Before flight training, both served tours in gunnery aboard cruisers—Snowden as gunnery officer in USS *West Virginia* and McCampbell as a gunnery observer in the scout plane assigned to USS *Portland*—where they mastered the geometry of calling shot—a skill that transferred almost seamlessly to aerial gunnery.

Both benefited from natural flying talent and by examples set by a few great aviator role models. After flight training, they served overlapping tours in Fighting Squadron Four in USS *Langley* (CV 4). There, piloting the Grumman F3F, with Snowden flying on the wing of a brilliant aerialist and squadron skipper LCDR Wendell Switzer, and McCampbell on the wing of a renowned aerial gunner, LTJG Joe Clifton, they honed their prowess in aerial combat.

Of Clifton, RADM Whitey Feightner, USN (Ret.) later commented, "He was always a great one for the troops. He'd get so excited (in briefings) tears would run down his cheeks. And the crew would have gone out and died for him right there."[8]

Snowden, imprinting more on Switzer's example, showed to be the better pilot at dive-bombing and McCampbell, under Clifton's tutelage, the better at aerial gunnery, skills that set their paths for later assignments.

In the earliest months of World War Two, both served in USS *Wasp* (CV-7) under Captain J.W. "Black Jack" Reeves, McCampbell as the ship's Landing Signal Officer, and Snowden as executive officer of embarked Scouting Squadron Seventy-Two. Snowden and McCampbell knew and observed each other, but more importantly had opportunity to closely observe Reeves and to appraise his leadership style for those traits that could be adopted. They saw in Reeves a commanding officer who could be vehemently outspoken, direct to the point of rudeness, "demanding on professional things...but the kind of skipper they'd want to go to war with."[9]

When *Wasp* transited from Atlantic to Pacific operations in 1942, the two had opportunity to assess and assimilate the leadership style of a new skipper, Captain Forrest Sherman. Sherman was more cerebral, having spent the better part of the prior three years as the CNO's aviation planner and in the fleet planning offices of OP-12 originating operational plans for an offensive carrier strategy in the Pacific.

Admiral Nimitz held Sherman in high regard for his strategic vision, but as well for his logic and ability to command an argument well above his rank in debate with flag officers.[10] That strength of personality translated to "cool, calm, and collected"[11] deportment when Sherman exercised precise ship-handling to back down fires after *Wasp* was torpedoed, and again when Sherman, McCampbell and Snowden, with the surviving crew of *Wasp*, abandoned ship in September 1942.

CDR McCampbell readies for another flight

From graduate instruction in the finer points of aeronautics and tactics, to the example of near polar opposites of leadership style exhibited by their *Wasp* skippers, the two grew into their own command personas that bridged both examples.

Know Your Men: The stress of prolonged combat operations presented both commanders with unique leadership situations apart from the two days of battle in June 1944 that showed them to be mindful of their personnel, and, in the event, had the effect of binding their people closer to them.

When, in November 1944 during repeated strikes on Japanese shipping in Ormoc Bay in the Philippines, three popular enlisted gunners from Air Group Fifteen's bombing squadron were killed, enlisted aircrews protested by refusing to fly more missions. Others joined in what amounted to mutiny that could have been construed as cowardice in the face of the enemy.

When bombing squadron commander Jim Mini informed air group commander McCampbell of the gunners' recalcitrant display on the flight deck, McCampbell sensed he could not directly face the group and thereby make the incident official. Such a confrontation would have removed any latitude he still held to resolve the issue by other than formal court-martial charges. McCampbell counseled Mini to inform the group he concurred with their position, and would henceforth remove the enlisted gunners from flying status, with loss of flight pay and with loss of any privilege of returning home early with the air group. McCampbell had Mini announce bombing missions would be flown with the gunner position empty, without the benefit of their service, thus exposing their pilots to greater personal risk.

Humbled and embarrassed, the enlisted gunners, as a group, withdrew their complaint.

SNAPSHOTS

"It was in this moment that Dave McCampbell most clearly demonstrated his leadership."[12] In that one episode, McCampbell proved himself a demanding yet compassionate disciplinarian, endearing himself to not just his officers, but enlisted aircrewmen as well.

Thirteen months before, Air Group Sixteen was striking Wake Island, reinforced by the Japanese since its capture in late 1941. Snowden was leading a third strike of the day guiding fifty-four aircraft of Lexington's air group against Wake installations when, on return to the ship, one of his SBD dive-bombers was forced down with engine damage at least fifty miles east of Wake in the direction of the task group.

Two aircraft covering the ditching site reported the pilot and gunner to be alive and in their raft, but had to depart the scene and return to the carrier when their fuel ran low. At that moment, the task group commander embarked in Lexington, wanting to quickly retire from the area, refused to permit any more launches of search aircraft to pinpoint the survivors for rescue.

The squadron officers were in near revolt at what they assumed was the admiral's disregard for their imperiled aircrewmen. Relying on their estimation of the air group commander's regard for his men, they approached Snowden *en masse* and urgently pleaded for his intervention.[13]

Snowden made his way to the flag bridge and asked for an audience with the admiral, whereupon he made a respectful but insistent case for launching an immediate flight to fix a location the downed crew. He won the admiral over and was permitted to conduct a search.

He recounted in his action report for that day,

I led a search flight for and found Lieutenant (JG) McCarthy and AOM2/c Bonilla, 102 miles from the ship. I kept one plane down low circling the boat (life raft) while I climbed to 8,000 feet and turned

*on my emergency IFF and also got communication
with the ship on high frequency. I then broadcasted
to the rescue vessel the latitude and longitude of
the rubber boat. I was ordered to return to the ship
and did so.*[14]

Within hours the survivors had drifted so far they could
not be located until three days later, when by happenstance,
the rescue submarine encountered them. In the moment,
however, and knowing well the urgency placed by aircrews
on exhausting all means for combat rescue, Snowden's
decisive action on behalf of this aircrew secured the fast
loyalty of the air group.

CDR Ernie Snowden

Bonilla, the rescued radioman-gunner, speaking on
behalf of the enlisted aircrewmen, perhaps captured the
feeling when remarking, "everyone loved the air group
commander. He was a pilot's pilot."[15]

Know Your Business: As carrier air group commanders in the late spring of 1944, McCampbell and Snowden
were well prepared to lead their groups into action in the
Philippine Sea, having amassed substantial combat hours

in the air and accumulated considerable experience in leading dozens of aircraft types in coordinated single and multi-group strikes. Their particular expertise, gathered over the course of their flying careers—for McCampbell, aerial gunnery; for Snowden, dive-bombing and ground attack—showed itself in the battle to come, but their penchant for leading from the front proved the greatest inspiration for their air group pilots and enlisted aircrews.

Very few possessed the skill for air combat maneuvering and the eye for deflection shooting that was instinctual for McCampbell. Fewer still were in such a commanding position to fully employ it. McCampbell didn't hesitate to assume the lead for the air group's fighter sweeps, strike escort, and combat air patrol missions that consistently placed him in the midst of opposing enemy aircraft. Results were swift in coming: McCampbell scored seven aerial victories in just two missions on the first day of the Turkey Shoot, becoming an ace in on day, and going on in the months that followed to tally thirty-four aerial victories.

"He was widely criticized by both superiors and contemporaries for having come down with 'Zero fever',"[16] prompting his task group commander to counsel him to stop carving notches other than in self-defense. Yet, those serving under McCampbell in Air Group Fifteen would point to the air group commander's performance as a source of pride and as a motivating factor.

"Having a CAG who was setting records in the air battles they were fighting..." inspired them to put forth similar effort in their own assignments. Air Group Fifteen's overall performance "demonstrated that McCampbell's inspirational leadership did have effect."[17]

On the day following Air Group Fifteen's and Sixteen's aerial victories of 19 June, an all-consuming focus of the task force was finding and eliminating the Japanese carrier fleet. Contact had been lost overnight, and concern grew that the Japanese were rapidly retiring to the west to open the distance and vouchsafe their escape from U.S. attack.

Air Group Sixteen Commander Snowden conceived a plan to configure F6F Hellcats with jettisonable belly tanks for extra fuel, to arm each with a five-hundred-pound bomb, and to launch on a maximum range 475 miles search for the Japanese carrier fleet.

Snowden approached the embarked task force commander, Vice Admiral Mitscher, to pitch the idea, receiving a tentative head nod of approval. Snowden beat a hasty exit from the flag bridge and made for Fighting Squadron Sixteen's ready room to find volunteers.

"Addressing the Airdales," he said. "Chances are less than fifty-fifty you'll get back." He chalked a dozen numbers on the blackboard with his name in the first spot. Thirty minutes later he returned to find every slot taken. Snowden was part of the reason for Lexington's sky-high morale."[18]

Admiral Burke was personally acquainted with McCampbell and Snowden. In his experience, those two fine air group commanders embodied the quintessence of strong leadership style under the harshest combat conditions. In practice, both McCampbell and Snowden were the exemplars of the injunction to Know Yourself, Know Your Men, and Know Your Business. They were leaders who, in Admiral Richardson's phrasing, "learned and adapted to achieve maximum possible performance" by displaying leadership traits that merit emulation in the naval service today.[19]

SNAPSHOTS

NOTES:

1.   Admiral Arleigh Burke U.S. Navy (Ret), *Young Officers and Leadership*, Thomas J. Cutler, ed. *Naval Leadership*, (Annapolis: Naval Institute Press, 2015), p 42.

2.   Admiral John M. Richardson, U.S. Navy, *A Design for Maintaining Maritime Superiority*, Version 1.0, January 2016, p 7.

3.   Thomas J. Cutler, ed. *Naval Leadership*, (Annapolis: Naval Institute Press, 2015) p 5.

4.   Thomas McKelvey Cleaver, *Fabled Fifteen* (Havertown, PA: Casemate, 2014) p 25.

5.   Major Thomas U. Wall, *USMC, Leadership: The Theory Behind the Principles*, U.S. Naval Institute *Proceedings*, (December 1976), pp 72-77.

6.   RADM James A. Winnefeld, Sr. USN (Ret.), *Career Compass: Navigating through the Navy's Officer Assignment and Promotion Systems*, Thomas J. Cutler, ed. *Naval Leadership*, (Annapolis: Naval Institute Press, 2015), pp 139-145.

7.   Major C.A. Bach, USA, *Know Your Men... Know Business... Know Yourself*, Thomas J. Cutler, ed. *Naval Leadership* (Annapolis: Naval Institute Press, 2015), pp 164-165.

8.   RADM Edward L. Feightner, USN (Ret.) in *Whitey* by Peter Mersky, (Annapolis: Naval Institute Press, 2014), p 109.

9.   Paul Stillwell, interviewer, *The Reminiscences of Captain David McCampbell, USN (Ret.)*, (Annapolis: U.S. Naval Institute, 2010), p 82.

10. Edward S. Miller, *War Plan Orange* (Annapolis: Naval Institute Press, 1991), p 221.

11. Paul Stillwell, interviewer, *The Reminiscences of Captain David McCampbell, USN (Ret.)*, (Annapolis: U.S. Naval Institute, 2010), p 107.

12. Cleaver, p 202.

13. AOM1/c Paul Bonilla, USN (Ret.), *A Long Way Back from Wake, Ernest Snowden*, interviewer, *Personal Reminiscences*, (2018).

14. LCDR Ernest Snowden, *Wake Mission Summary.* AG16/A16–3 Serial 194. November 3, 1943.

15. Bonilla.

16. Cleaver, p 26.

17. Ibid.

18. Barrett Tillman, *Clash of the Carriers*, (New York: Penguin Group, 2005), pp 204-205.

19. Richardson, p 8.

SNAPSHOTS

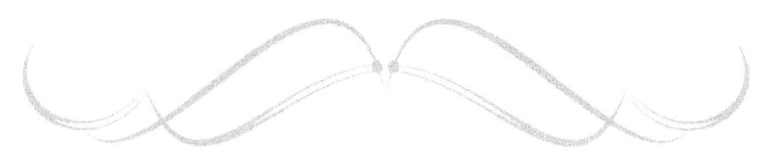

ERNEST SNOWDEN IS A 1970 graduate of the U.S. Naval Academy and a former naval aviator. After active duty, he continued in the naval reserve as an aeronautical engineering duty officer until his retirement in 2000.

He worked for a succession of private companies including *Cessna* Aircraft and *General Electric* before joining *Northrop Grumman Corporation*, where for thirty years he guided strategic planning and new business capture for manned and unmanned naval aircraft programs.

In retirement, he serves as a volunteer docent at the Smithsonian, conducting tours of the Air and Space Museum. He holds a BS in marketing from the University of West Florida and Masters of Business Administration from the University of Georgia.

His first published work, *Winged Brothers*, was presented a silver medal award by MWSA, and his second work, *Maritime Unmanned*, a bronze medal award.

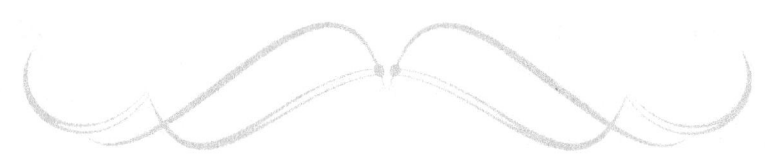

FOURTH OF JULY

Connie Cockrell

ERNIE LAY ON HIS BACK in bed, left arm under his head propped up on a pillow. He took a drag from the first cigarette of the day as he watched the daylight grow stronger through the pulled shade of the tiny camper he lived in.

He jumped at the sound of poppers in the dirt road that ran past the front of his trailer. A glance at the clock made him groan. Seven-thirty in the morning and the little brats were already out playing with fireworks.

He flung the sweaty sheet away and stood up. It was a single short step to the screened window. After he pulled the shade aside and winced from the full brunt of the early morning sun in hung-over eyes, he yelled, "Knock it off," then slammed the window shut.

Ernie sighed. That was just going make it hotter in the camper, but he couldn't take the constant pop, pop, popping. It sounded too much like gunfire.

The ashes from his cigarette, still between two nicotine-stained fingers, dropped to join the remains of its brethren on the lifeless carpet beside the bed.

In what passed for a kitchen he scooped coffee into the maker and filled it with water. He punched the start button and was made slightly less grumpy at the sound of water beginning its path through the fresh grounds.

SNAPSHOTS

Shouts of warning rang out from the road outside—the kids had set another string of poppers alight. Ernie braced. *Pop, pop, pop, pop, pop*, in rapid succession with screams of glee coming from the now larger pack of kids gathered from the trailer park.

He stared out of the tiny window over the sink at the trailer next door, smoking a cigarette and waiting for the coffee.

He wanted to get out of town, get to the country, someplace without parades, crowds, or fireworks but the car was in the shop.

Before the coffee was done, he poured some into his least dirty cup, letting the still brewing coffee pour over the hot plate, hissing and steaming and adding to the burnt coffee smell. He shoved the pot back under the stream and sipped the life blood of his day. His nerves were already on edge from the popping and screaming outside.

When the phone rang, he jumped. Who the hell is calling at five till eight? He picked up the cell phone lying on the table amidst the remains of takeout wrappers, bags, and empty cans of beer.

"What?" he snarled.

"Good morning to you, too, buddy," the voice responded with a laugh.

"It's too early, Brian." Ernie scrubbed the cigarette out in the overflowing ashtray next to the loveseat. He put his coffee on the stained arm of the sofa and plopped his feet on the coffee table, scattering more take-out wrappers. "The damn kids are outside already, firing off poppers and screaming like the Viet Cong."

"Come on out to the house, brother. I've got brats and ribs and Mary's made potato salad. No fireworks, I promise."

Ernie's interest picked up. His brother, Brian had the childhood home, an old farmhouse they grew up in. He swallowed some of the still too hot coffee. "Car's in the shop."

"I'll come get you. I know how the fourth brings out your PTSD. Say yes."

Ernie lit another cigarette with his *Zippo*—his engraved unit crest nearly rubbed away. A screamer went off. It sounded like it was right outside his trailer. He dove for the floor, coffee flew all over the loveseat and ragged carpet.

A tinny voice came from the phone, now on the floor just under the kitchen cabinet. "Ernie? Ernie? What was that? Are you okay?"

Face flushed with shame, Ernie got up and retrieved the phone. "Yeah, I'm all right. Damn kids set off a screamer."

He walked back to the loveseat and picked up his cup. He poured more coffee into it and shoved the kitchen table wrappers off onto the floor to sit down at the table.

"Are you coming out?"

"Yeah," Ernie scrubbed his three-day-old beard. If he stayed here much longer those kids would be dead. "Yeah. Come and get me. I'll be cleaned up by the time you get here."

When Brian arrived in his new SUV, Ernie was sitting outside his camper, shaved and in clean clothes, smoking. Brian got out and gave his brother a hug. "I don't see any kids."

"I chased 'em off."

"Glad you're coming out. Mary made your favorite, lemon meringue pie."

The two of them got into the car. "You two are too good to me. I'm a mess."

SNAPSHOTS

"That's what family is for, Ernie. You did your duty, time for us to pay it back."

Ernie stared out of the passenger window as his younger brother backed out of the parking spot.

The camper was rusted and ugly. The lawn chair he'd been sitting in was missing half of the webbing. He could still hear the pop, pop, popping of gunfire deep in his memory and if he took his hands off his knees, they'd be shaking.

He felt the way his camper looked.

"Thanks, Brian. I appreciate that."

A TWENTY-YEAR AIR FORCE CAREER, time as a manager at a computer operations company, wife, mother, sister, and volunteer, provides a rich background for Connie Cockrell's storytelling.

Cockrell grew up in upstate New York, just outside of Gloversville, before she joined the military at age eighteen. Having lived in Europe, Great Britain, and several places around the United States, she now lives in Payson, Arizona with her husband—hiking, gardening, and playing Bunko.

She writes about whatever comes into her head so her books could be in any genre. She's published twenty books so far, has been included in five different anthologies and been published online.

Connie's always on the lookout for a good story idea. Beware, you may be the next one.

She can be found at:

https://www.facebook.com/ConniesRandomThoughts

LIVING WITH AN ALIEN

Jim Tritten

T HE FEDERAL GOVERNMENT, ESPECIALLY THE military, has specific rules regarding to whom they grant security clearances and access to classified information. As a retired commander in the Navy, I have never begrudged the powers that be the right to make those rules. So, when I moved in with Jasmine, my then-girlfriend, in 1990, I dutifully reported the event to our Special Security Officer (SSO) at the Naval Postgraduate School in Monterey, California.

I worked there as a Department of the Navy civil service employee and faculty member. Rules required me to report contacts with any foreign nationals. You see, when I met her, Jasmine was a citizen of Denmark, lawfully in the United States as a legal immigrant in possession of a coveted green card, identifying her as a Permanent Resident Alien.

The SSO interviewed both Jasmine and me, and frankly, I did not think it would be a problem. After all, it had been many hundreds of years since marauding bands of Vikings with horned helmets roamed the North Atlantic in search of treasures and young virginal maidens.

But when the SSO asked me if Jasmine intended to become a U.S. citizen, and I replied, "No," I saw a red flag raised in her eyes and body language.

SNAPSHOTS

I suddenly realized it was going to be difficult after all. And with that difficulty came a very real and huge problem. Keeping a Special Compartmented Information (SCI) security clearance was a condition of my employment as a Department of the Navy professor. Without an SCI clearance, I could not keep my job.

Jasmine was very clear about not wanting to become an American citizen. Apparently, Denmark would automatically revoke her birth citizenship there if she swore allegiance to any foreign nation. They did not mind if she lived her entire life outside the kingdom or if she held the status of a permanent resident of another country. But no dual citizenship for any Danes.

That was a tough nut to crack, and I was not going to even try with someone with whom I had only recently started to share living arrangements. I did my best to explain why Jasmine did not wish to become an American citizen to the SSO. She wrote it all down.

Some months went by, and I heard nothing from the Navy. Now hearing "nothing" from the bureaucracy is not necessarily a good sign. I had other things on my mind— like teaching classes and, oh yes, proposing to Jasmine. So, after she said, "Yes," I went to the SSO again. I reported that my live-in girlfriend was now my fiancée, and we intended to get married in about six weeks.

That SSO was not the same person to whom I turned in the original paperwork. There had been a transfer of personnel. To my amazement, the new SSO had no record of anything in her files regarding me living with an alien and why that foreigner declined American citizenship. The new SSO acknowledged my update for my SCI clearance and continued access [and ability to keep my job] was still being settled in Washington.

"No records?"

"No."

She asked me if I was concerned about anything. Obviously, there had not been a complete turnover with the former SSO.

I explained I was living with an alien and trying to comply with the regulations. I got the routine question about Jasmine intending to become a U.S. citizen. When I replied, "No," I again saw the red flag in the new SSO's eyes and her body language.

I pushed. "So, you have no record I came in and reported living with an alien, let alone the multitude of reasons Jasmine gave why she was not going to pursue citizenship?"

"No. Whatever you turned in was sent to Washington. We have no record of it here." She then suggested I prepare a written memorandum on the issues and submit them to her. Upon receipt, she would send it off to be added to my case, still in Washington for adjudication.

The following is a verbatim copy of the memorandum that I submitted to a bureaucracy that is not known for its sense of humor.

NOVEMBER 27, 1990

MEMORANDUM

FROM: ASSOCIATE PROFESSOR JAMES TRITTEN

TO: SPECIAL SECURITY OFFICER

SUBJ: SCI CLEARANCE

As requested, this memo will explain the citizenship status and intentions of my fiancée, Ms. Jette (a.k.a. Jasmine) Clark, with regard to my retention of an SCI clearance and access. Ms. Clark and I now intend to be married on December 29, 1990, and we have been living together since March 1990.

As a citizen of Denmark, my fiancée remains eligible for Danish social security retirement and

*health benefits from that nation even if she never
pays into the system and never lives in Denmark.
These benefits would be a modest pension, but more
importantly, free socialized medicine and lifetime
care in a state-run old age home. If I were to move
to Denmark with Jasmine, apparently upon my own
retirement, I would also be eligible for the free
socialized medicine as well since I would be the
spouse of a Danish subject.*

*Furthermore, as a taxpayer in the United States,
my fiancée will be eligible for U.S. Social Security
benefits. The United States has recently signed a
treaty with the Kingdom of Denmark to allow U.S.
Social Security benefits to be paid to the beneficia-
ries that reside in Denmark and derivative Danish
social security benefits as her spouse.*

From what we can tell, there are only two benefits
from Jasmine becoming a U.S. citizen. First, she would
have the right to vote. Second, she would have the right
to serve on juries in U.S. courts. I am not sure that the
second is an inducement to citizenship.

All things considered, I cannot, with a clear conscience,
recommend to Jasmine that she give up her citizenship that
she has had for forty-eight years—twenty-four of them
while in the U.S. We should not forget that Denmark is a
nation allied militarily with the United States in NATO
and one which has special treaty ties with our nation.

Ms. Clark has agreed to be investigated by the appropriate agencies if she has not already been so.

Jasmine and I were married on December 29, 1990, in
the chapel of the Naval Postgraduate School in Monterey,
California.

On the 1st of May 1991, the SSO called me to her office
and informed me the Navy had granted an exception on
April 11th and my current clearance and access to SCI

were continued. I breathed a big sigh of relief because it meant I would be able to keep my job. I did not understand why it had taken three weeks to inform me, but I skedaddled out of her office before I heard anything I did not want to hear.

I went home and asked Jasmine if she recalled being interviewed by the Navy, filling out forms that drilled into her background, and my discussion about the relationship between security clearances, the investigation that would be conducted on her, and my ability to keep my job. She said she did.

I told Jasmine the Navy had made up their minds and that, "we can stay married."

Jasmine let out a sigh of relief. Then she screwed up her face and asked me, "What would you have done if they said, 'No'?"

I told her I had learned a few years ago not to answer theoretical questions from wives. I also confessed the Navy really did not use the phrase, "we could stay married," but instead, I was going to keep my security clearance and hence my job. Explaining what an exception was fell into the category of too much information.

The SSO had also informed me I would not have to get a new exception with each new periodic update of my clearance, but I would occasionally be required to submit new paperwork on my wife. I promised to keep my eye on her.

Over the years, I changed jobs from time to time, always remaining within the Department of the Navy civil service system. I reported living with an alien to each new SSO at each new location. There was never any problem. They had her in their files.

In 2002, I took a senior job with a Department of Defense (DoD) Agency in New Mexico. For the uninitiated, the Department of the Navy is a part of the DoD.

SNAPSHOTS

The new job also depended upon my ability to keep an SCI clearance. When I came up for another periodic review in 2005, I was not particularly surprised to get a phone call from one of the folks that did background checks on people being reviewed for security clearances. The calls regularly occurred, and I was frequently required to give input to individuals who worked for me or knew.

This time, the agent wanted to discuss "my case."

What case?

I met with an investigator at a local restaurant. He did not want to meet with me in either my office on the base or at my home with my wife. Nice guy. We made small talk. Then he said, "What is this about you living with a foreign national?"

Shocked, I explained to him I had been doing so since 1990, reported it at the time, and for each periodic update. Furthermore, the Navy granted an exception fourteen years ago and renewed the exception for each update.

He smiled and said, "Whatever the Navy did is of no concern to the department of defense. You now worked for us."

He continued by explaining they were going to start all over again. Both Jasmine and I would have to fill out all new paperwork, and then the DoD would adjudicate the impact of my living arrangement on whether I was going to be able to keep a security clearance... and my job.

I went through the whole history with him in great detail. I once again saw in his eyes and body language that a red flag was raised when I explained that Jasmine did not intend to become a U.S. citizen.

I went home, searched through my old files, and found I had kept a copy of the original 1990 memorandum to the Navy SSO. I gave a copy to the investigator at our next meeting. I told him if the DoD did not accept the previous adjudication by the Navy and my previous explanation, they could do what they wanted with my case. If necessary, I would seek employment elsewhere.

Brave words from someone who was not yet retirement eligible and had a new thirty-year mortgage on a home in New Mexico.

I received an e-mail from the DoD agency SSO on July 21, 2006, informing me I could once again stay married to Jasmine. Well, they did not use those exact words, but that was how I explained it to Jasmine, again.

Years later, after I retired from the federal government, Jasmine and I learned Denmark had changed their rules, and as far as they were concerned, she could have dual citizenship. Jasmine applied and was sworn in as a Naturalized American citizen on May 23, 2017.

She surrendered her green card—a status she held for fifty-two years. She obtained an American passport and retained her Danish passport.

I am fully retired from work and no longer have any obligation to anyone to report living with an alien... which, of course, I no longer do.

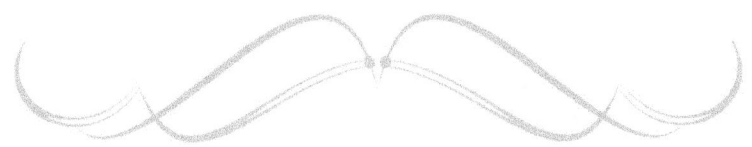

J IM TRITTEN IS A RETIRED naval aviator residing in a semi-rural village in New Mexico with his Danish author/artist wife and three cats.

GLIMPSES OF THE WAR EFFORT AT HOME

Cynthia Baughan Wheaton

I N WORLD WAR II, OUR military was fighting abroad for freedom. At home, hundreds of thousands of workers were returning the favor, working to support our military. My parents were two who contributed on the home front. This is their story.

THE WEDDING – MAY 24, 1941

Despite her jittery stomach, Margaret was radiant in her flowing white gown. Jackson was glowing with pride, looking handsome in his formal black tuxedo. The future was unknown, but today they would focus on their love and commitment.

SNAPSHOTS

America was not yet officially at war, but circumstances around the world were deteriorating. Already, many European citizens and soldiers had suffered brutality and deprivation.

My parents knew about hard times. On their wedding day, they were in their late twenties, having lived through the Great War and Great Depression, and experienced in juggling their lives and resources.

When Jackson was a child, his father died in a freak accident, one of his brothers died from tetanus, and he almost lost another brother to the Spanish Flu. As a young man, Jackson left the family farm to join the Civilian Conservation Corps—his salary paid directly to his widowed mother.

In her youth, Margaret's family moved yearly, trying to find something better, or cheaper. Margaret could not accept a college scholarship because her parents had no money to help. Shortly after high school, in 1933, my mother acquired much-desired skills in typing and shorthand.

Now, on their wedding day, the older-than-average bride and groom celebrated with loved ones in the city they called home—Richmond, Virginia. They had saved for a small, but meaningful, event. The candlelit church wedding was followed by cake and punch at Margaret's sister's cozy home, where all seven of Margaret's family members had lived since her mother's death. Margaret and Jackson were married at last.

Later, seated in an uncharacteristically fancy restaurant, the bride looked down at the menu. To her horror, a trickle of going-away rice poured from her hat onto her lap. Embarrassment turned to smiles. They could hardly eat, thinking about their new life together. Margaret knew she would always be strengthened by having my father's caring and muscular arms around her. Jackson knew he had a true partner for life.

PEARL HARBOR DAY – DECEMBER 7, 1941

My parents heard of the devastating attack on Pearl Harbor as they left church. Like everyone else, they knew America was at war. Both of my parents wanted to help the war effort at home rather than have Jackson choose immediate enlistment. Jack's identical twin brother would be an integral part of their plan.

Originally, when the twins had moved to Richmond from the farm, they determined Lee would get a job, while Jackson went to trade school. Jack would learn home building skills, including drafting and surveying, then start a business with Lee as a working partner.

They joined the Richmond Blues, forerunner of the Virginia National Guard. In 1938, their company had won the national Musketry Trophy.

Lee volunteered to head to Newport News, a few hours away, to get a job in the rapidly expanding naval shipyard. Once he achieved that goal, he would help Jack do the same.

SNAPSHOTS

Those were not the only plans required. Margaret and Jack needed to find a renter for the 1836-square-foot, three-bedroom, one-bath honeymoon home he had lovingly built for them. It had felt like a dream to own their brand-new home. They wanted it to be well cared for by responsible tenants in their absence. Their car had to be moved to a safe place where, due to the expected scarcity of gasoline and frequently needed tires, it could be put up on blocks until the war's end.

"The House That Jack Boil..."

Finally, Margaret had a particular request. While many married couples wanted to start a family before they could be separated, my mother did not want to experience pregnancy and early child-rearing without her husband. My father adored children and did not want to miss out on watching his own grow up. They agreed to wait, hoping his draft status would not change.

With a plan in place, Jack began to focus on maximizing his income, despite the difficult-to-predict world of self-employment. Margaret continued her current job, saving as much as possible.

NECESSARY SEPARATION – FEB AND MARCH 1942

Jackson went to Newport News, looking for a job and housing. The realities of the high-demand rental market started to lower their expectations. Employees flooded the shipyard, ultimately from 8,000 to over 43,000.

Thanks to the train between Richmond and Newport News, there were many trips back and forth—and even more letters. Mail was delivered twice daily, so a letter sent in the morning could be delivered that afternoon. Their only complaint was missing each other. Their hope was to rent a home similar in size, move their belongings in, and stay until they could return home.

February 2, 1942,

Newport News, Virginia

Dear Margaret,

...Seems like a dream that we have been separated but I think we are doing the right thing. We will be together again....

I haven't been able to find out a thing about a flat. I am pretty sure we can get something though. Do hope we can rent our house alright and to a good party. I don't think we will be able to get what we want down here but we can get as good as the average person down here has been able to get.

With all my love, Jack

* * *

Monday 3/2/42,

Richmond, Virginia

My Own Dear Husband,

SNAPSHOTS

[The realtor] said that we certainly should be able to get $50.00 [rental income]

...Have decided I will tell [her employer] that I'm leaving April 1.

[Realtor] said he could rent the house in 5 minutes but he knew we wanted good tenants and would look around and try to find a good one. Said he could sell ours tomorrow but I told him the answer to that was still "No."

...Just got in from a [social gathering]. Everyone there was very surprised to hear we were moving....

* * *

February 4, 1942,

Newport News

Dear Sweetheart,

Do not have any encouraging report about a place to rent. There are a plenty of new houses but all are for sale $500.00 and about $47.00 per month, we just can't get one of those. There are a plenty of apartments being built but there are thousands of applications for them. I found we wouldn't have any selection at all. The way they rent down here is first come first serve. They won't hold a thing for you. We will get something though. Maybe you and I can rent 2 rooms somewhere and wait until we can find something better. The Real Estate places close so early I don't have much chance to see them. Maybe we could put our names on a list for a certain apartment and hope for the best.

Your husband, Jack

On February 24, 1942, Jackson moved to Newport News to look for full time work, despite the lack of a housing. Right away, he was hired by Newport News Shipbuilding & Drydock in the Joiner Department. Those skilled craftsmen and carpenters joined bulkheads and finished living spaces, often working in cramped, even dangerous, spaces.

February 24, 1942

My darling wife,

...I figure that I was lucky to get on [i.e., hired] today and wouldn't have had it not been for Lee. Lee went in and asked the man to take me. I will not start at such a great salary but will make I think $40.35 per week six days of course that will be every week and he promised me a $.10 raise in about a month. They are deferring the boys from the draft. I am staying at the same place with Lee and eating with him too.

I have missed you so much and our nice new home but I guess I will have to make some sacrific-es. Well, I will start tomorrow on the greatest job in the world. I think I will like it. Think perhaps Lee and I may work together but don't know yet.

Your loving husband, Jack

* * *

March 9, 1942

Dearest Margaret,

I think I have found a place but won't know defi-nitely until tomorrow. The layout is on the back. It *is on a very nice street and is a very nice apt, but it is not new by any means. It has oil heat furnished gas range and refrigerator and rents for $45...it is better than I expected we would be able to get.*

An officer's wife lives in it now and her husband is at Pearl Harbor. She is going to take the one-bedroom across the hall on the first of April. She said they were at Pearl Harbor the morning of the bombing and that her husband was still here. She said that she had a telephone that she only used to talk to her husband once a week as it cost $12.00 each time she talked to him.

I am doing my best,

Your husband, Jack

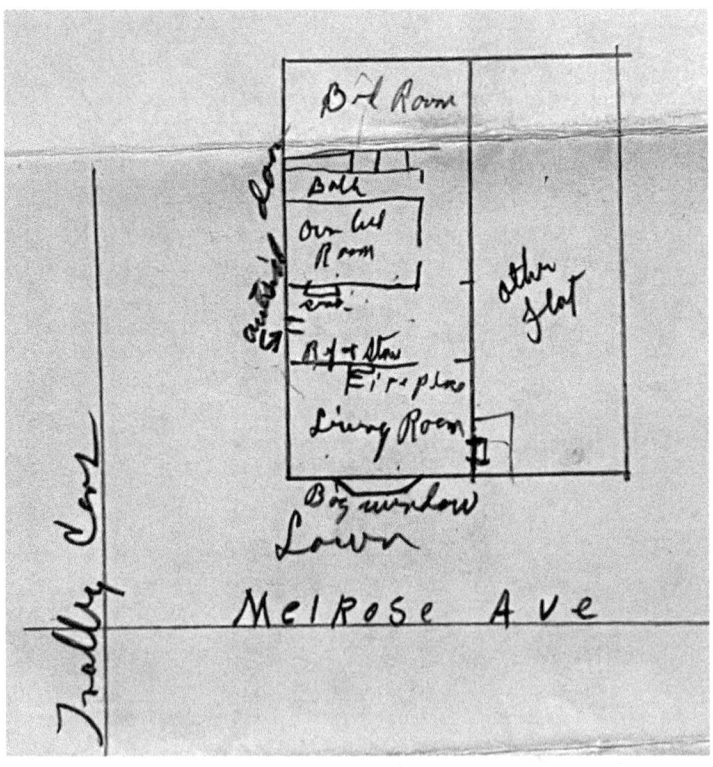

3/11/42

Richmond, VA

Dear Jack,

Just got your letter about the apartment...Like you, I believe it is better than we could hardly expect to get. The lay-out is fine and if you think it is satisfactory, it is ok with me. I'm glad heat, stove and refrig are furnished. That saves us additional expense.

I am right excited about it since it will be definitely private. That means a lot. Do hope the deal went through. I feel brighter than I have since you left – in fact I'm anxious now for the weekend to come so that I can go with you to see it.

If the question of our home is settled, we can really have a second honeymoon. Good work sweetheart.

All my love, Margaret

* * *

3/12/42

My Dear Husband,

...I miss you so much! I hate to leave Richmond but my heart is where you are and I cannot be completely happy without you....

Love + Kisses, Margaret

* * *

SNAPSHOTS

March 24, 1942

My dear Ten Months old Bride,

In 1942 Remember "May 24th" 1941 with Love.

Remember Pearl Harbor too.

...Have been building ships all day and I am really getting to be a ship builder. Have been sore all day from that heavy lifting. I think I strained a muscle in my arm as I have hardly been able to lift it all day....

Love, Jack, The Groom

TOGETHER AGAIN – APRIL 1942

Margaret had carefully packed up their belongings, storing whatever they would not be able to squeeze into their apartment. The Hampton rental was much smaller than their honeymoon house. Margaret arrived in the bustling port by train, but their large items were shipped directly to the apartment. Safely tucked away, Margaret had a strong reference letter from her employer. Her skills would be needed by someone, she was sure of it.

She had long ago accepted the fact that Jackson was a quiet man, speaking few words. He had an engaging chuckle, however, and his letters to her had spoken deeply of love and longing. Now she would finally be in his arms again.

Margaret was soon faced with their new reality. Jackson was at work, and Lee answered the door, welcoming her. She had been given little warning they would be sharing space with Jack's twin, but there were no available alternatives. Her husband thankfully left her a special welcome. Just inside the door, he had placed his shirt, tie, jacket and hat on the back of a chair, simulating a personal greeting from him.

There was a note:

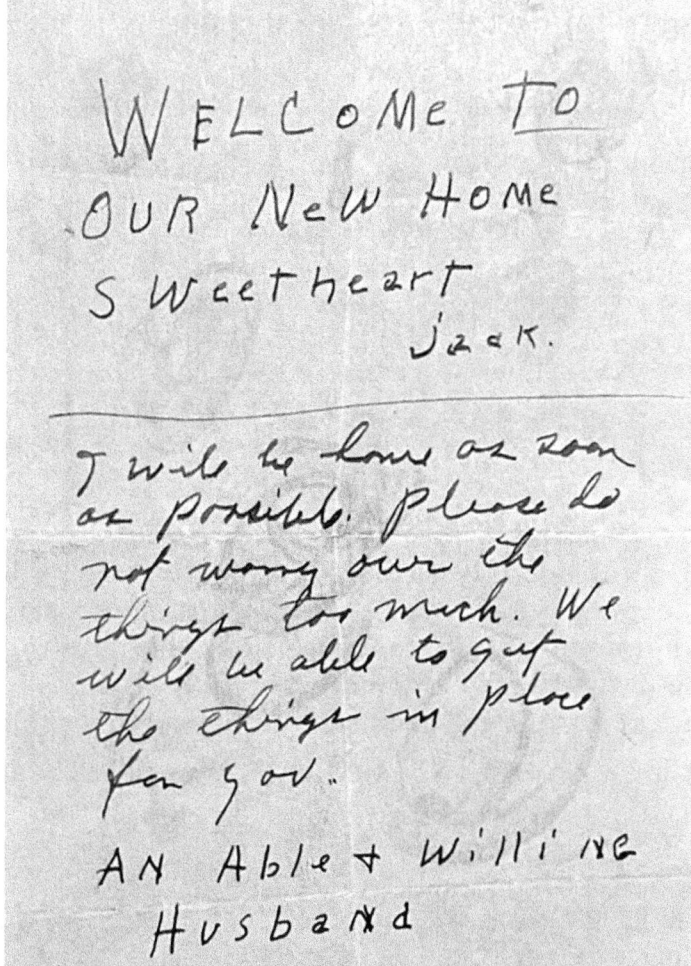

Together, though not completely alone, they were home.

SETTLING IN

Margaret and Jack (and Lee) must have been deeply concerned, because the outcome of the war was far from certain. They heard the first-hand story of the Pearl Harbor attack from their new neighbor, Lena Pettet.

SNAPSHOTS

Life was quickly changing. Rubber had been rationed since January, and sugar and gasoline were added in May. The ration system required time and energy to correctly manage.

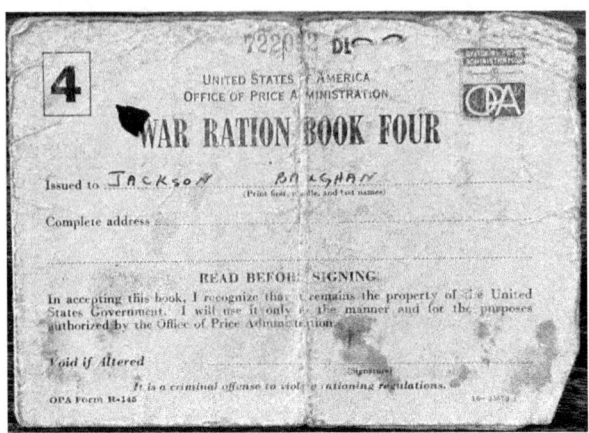

Margaret initially focused on the demanding job of housekeeping and enjoyed sharing chore time with Lena. When not using public transportation, Margaret rode her bicycle to the library and markets, appreciating the benefits of exercise. Her special treat was window shopping.

On a quick trip to visit family she noted wartime activity:

9/23/42

My Dearest Jack,

I'm writing this on the train...Hampton is sending about 50 draftees to Richmond on this same train. They were all laughing and talking at the station and taking it in their stride....

Your loving wife, Margaret

Routine Life

Life took on a steady pattern. Mail fortunately continued to be quickly delivered but few photos were taken. Family visits were rare and only when there was money for train tickets. Lee sometimes stayed in Norfolk with their sister, the wife of a naval officer.

Given the high-value targets in the area, blackout curtains were required. Lee was drafted, then deferred. Jack received his draft notice, but then received continual deferments. What kept them on the home-front was their work at the shipyard—perhaps in combination with their age.

News was slow but relished. Jack and Margaret listened to the radio, including speeches by President Roosevelt, and soaked up the newsreels shown in theaters before each featured movie. Too frequently, news came of those lost or injured. Depression claimed victims in a time when few people understood mental health challenges.

Just as in their youth, my parents focused on putting one foot in front of the other. On October 31, 1942, Margaret wrote, "It is Halloween but no public demonstration allowed due to fear of saboteurs."

On November 6, she noted, "Encouraging news from the Egyptian front. The English seem to have Axis on the run!"

Starting in November 1943, Margaret no longer recorded her thoughts on the war or their personal activities.

Margaret and Jack joined a church and attended whenever they could. They made many close friends. Well-worn Bibles testify to the role of faith in their lives. On sunny days, they enjoyed local parks with friends from work or church, and rare vacations were spent visiting family.

Physical work at the noisy shipyard could be challenging, and overtime was common. Constant vigilance against error or sabotage was critical. Although accidents were rare at the Newport News shipyard, fifteen men died on April 27, 1944, while updating the USS *Saturn*. Eight of them were joiners, like Jackson.

Newport News
Shipbuilding & Drydock
Co.

Jackson
Baughan
1942

Starting in February 1943, Margaret worked in the payroll section at the Langley Memorial Aeronautical Laboratory, which was part of the National Advisory Committee for Aeronautics (NACA), the forerunner of NASA.

Sitting at a manual typewriter all day, documenting both positive and sad personnel changes could be stressful. Margaret fortunately accumulated many friends among her co-workers.

On September 16, 1944, Margaret was asked by NACA to immediately "increase her bond allotment to at least fifteen percent of her new salary."

She and Jack believed in the importance of bonds and regularly invested. It had been only three months since D-Day, so they knew there was stiff fighting ahead.

THE ACCIDENT

One evening after dark, Lena fell, and fractured her arm. Margaret knew it needed immediate medical attention to stop the bleeding and minimize the chance of infection.

Margaret's place-of-work at nearby Langley Field included a medical facility. There were strict blackout rules, and the night was dark. Jack got behind the wheel of Lena's car, waited a quick moment for his eyes to adjust, and drove into the night.

There were no traffic lights, no streetlights, and no headlights. The clear night sky did have some moonlight, but it was difficult to drive quickly and avoid an accident.

When they arrived at the base, Margaret—thanks to her credentials—was allowed in with her clearly-injured friend. Meanwhile, Jackson sat under armed guard just outside the gate.

Margaret teased him for decades that his naturally heavy beard, unshaved since morning, had made the guards suspicious. The patient was released hours later, and the three companions made the surreal journey back home.

JOURNEY TO BOSTON – MAY 1945

When Jack's sister Louise began planning a May wedding, the family had no idea how much there would be to celebrate. Then, Adolf Hitler committed suicide on April 30, with VE Day quickly following on May 8, marking the official end of WWII in Europe.

Jack and Margaret, Lee, and their younger brother, Fred, and his wife pooled their ration coupons and drove Louise to Boston for her nuptials with a young Navy officer.

Despite frequent tire blow-outs, the travelers arrived in time with celebration-worthy clothes. All of them were glowing with joy.

SNAPSHOTS

GOING HOME – SEPTEMBER 1945

The Japanese officially surrendered on September 9, 1945. The wartime effort, however, had started to wind down earlier. Margaret resigned her position effective August 18, with four weeks of paid leave.

She soon discovered that their honeymoon house was unlivable because of damage caused by a tenant. Therefore, a rental home had to be secured.

Wartime frugality had paid off when my parents restarted their life in Richmond. They had invested in war bonds and accumulated some savings—which they deposited in a Richmond bank on September 1. Thus, they had a small but critical head start on rebuilding a home and a business.

Life was not always easy. Margaret and Jack built a house close to family, had two healthy daughters, and established a successful business with brothers Lee and Fred.

They appreciated life without foreign threats, freedom to follow their dreams, and opportunities to help others. They were finally home to stay.

SNAPSHOTS

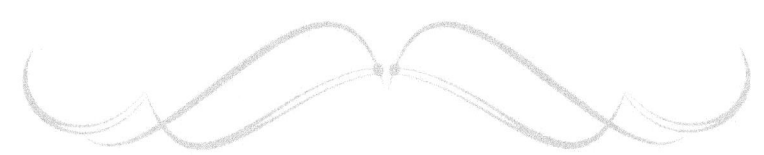

C YNTHIA BAUGHAN WHEATON'S LIFE HAS been steeped in history and respect for the military. Cynthia and her husband nurtured their two children into purpose-driven adulthood while building their own successful business and working together from home.

Her concise and readable book, *Are You Ready to Start Your Own Business? A Sanity Check for Those Who Dream of Self-Employment*, has been used at two colleges. Her second book, *Make Your Home Office Work*, will be available in 2024.

Find out more at: www.TheEntrepreneursFriend.com.

TEARS ON THE LETTER

Barbara Ellen Perkins Bazor, Ed.D

S HE OPENED THAT OLD CHEST drawer. Under a bundle of shabby clothes, her trembling hand felt that old envelope hidden for years like it was trying to tuck under some memories.

She took a deep breath as if trying to gain the courage to release the letter from its unsealed wrapping.

Gently, her weary hands held onto the letter that had repeatedly punctured a dagger into her heart. She held it tightly, but before she could attempt to read it again—since this was not the first time, she pressed the letter on her chest. And there, she helplessly let go of a soft whimper, leading to heavy drops of tears trickling down, drenching the letter once more.

Like many other times, the letter collected her tears and then dried them inside its envelope. She was still hurting. The memories never left. The memories lingered. They were painfully locked up in that letter. But she treasured that letter regardless of how it mistreated her. It was the same letter where she had found comfort and solace amid her loneliness.

The letter was all she got to feel his nearness. He had been gone for seven years now. The calendar reminded her that today was the day that the letter rested in the palm of her hand. Unforgettably, she had to rehearse the familiar pain that she couldn't get used to. Impossible.

SNAPSHOTS

She finally mustered herself to read the letter. But every word in it was censured in her mind. She had already memorized everything in that letter, just like her heart had always remembered him for years.

How he warmly called her "Mama".

Dear Mama,

When you're reading this letter, I should already be in heaven. I wished I could have stayed longer, but my life was long enough for me to live. I fought for freedom, for our country, and for you. I wanted you to be proud of me—your little Hero. You named me for that reason. But you see, Mama, I was not little anymore. I made the choice to join the military because I wanted my life to have meaning. I was hardheaded, I know, after all the years I put you through.

But there were other things I'd learned that I never thought I could do—that I could go on for days without sleeping but remain alert behind enemy lines. And I didn't fear death even though it was staring at me. And not coming home to you was not a bad thing because I was going home to my Creator. Even though I'm gone now, I wanted you to know how much I love you. And I promise you, Mama, I'll be good while waiting for you up here.

With Much Love,

Sgt. Hero Harry Johnson

Your son

After reading the letter, a smile lit up her face. She put the letter on her lips and whispered, "I love you, son. And you will always be my little Hero."

Gently, she folded the letter, inserted it back into its envelope, and tucked it away under his old clothes. Then she unlocked the door and opened it wide as she stood there, expecting him to appear from a distance.

He was there somewhere. She just knew it in her heart.

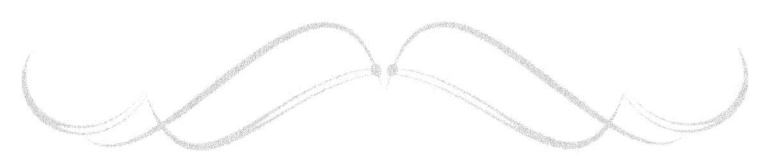

B ARBARA ELLEN PERKINS BAZOR, ED.D is a public
educator with twelve years of classroom experience
in Montgomery public schools (Alabama) and on
her eighth year as an instructional leader in Bibb County
school district, Macon, Georgia.

Recently, she was nominated for the Georgia
Association of Secondary School Principals (GASSP):
Assistant Principal of the Year Award 2020, a program
designed to recognize the outstanding leadership of active,
front-line assistant principals. She was placed in the top
five among all middle and high school assistant principals in Georgia.

Dr. Bazor served in the Army National Guard from
1997 to 2004 in Hawaii and Alabama. She earned her
doctorate in Educational Leadership, Policy, and Law
from Alabama State University in 2009.

Her latest book, *Subic: A Sailor's Memoir* (based on
the story of Bobby Earl Perkins), unveils a little-known
account of her father and his fellow servicemen who
endured racial discrimination in the military while stationed in Subic Bay Naval Base, Philippines during the
late 1960s.

Her works include *54 Poems for the Lord in 2 Days*,
The Joys Within, and *In the Presence of the Ultimate: A
Guide to Spiritual Inquiry*.

Dr. Bazor is married to James Kent Bazor, enjoying the
southern lifestyle, they call Montgomery, Alabama home.

375